The Censorship Issue

ISSUES
(formerly Issues for the Nineties)

Volume 27

Editor

Craig Donnellan

Independence
Educational Publishers
Cambridge

First published by Independence
PO Box 295
Cambridge CB1 3XP
England

British Library Cataloguing in Publication Data
The Censorship Issue – (Issues Series)
I. Donnellan, Craig II. Series
363.3'1

ISBN 1 86168 180 1

Printed in Great Britain
The Burlington Press
Cambridge

Typeset by
Claire Boyd

Cover
The illustration on the front cover is by
Pumpkin House.

CONTENTS

Chapter One: The Debate

Chapter Two: Sex and Violence

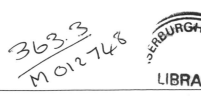

Introduction

The Censorship Issue is the twenty-seventh volume in the **Issues** series. The aim of this series is to offer up-to-date information about important issues in our world.

The Censorship Issue covers the debate over censorship and examines the issue of sex and violence on television and film.

The information comes from a wide variety of sources and includes:
Government reports and statistics
Newspaper reports and features
Magazine articles and surveys
Literature from lobby groups
and charitable organisations.

It is hoped that, as you read about the many aspects of the issues explored in this book, you will critically evaluate the information presented. It is important that you decide whether you are being presented with facts or opinions. Does the writer give a biased or an unbiased report? If an opinion is being expressed, do you agree with the writer?

The Censorship Issue offers a useful starting-point for those who need convenient access to information about the many issues involved. However, it is only a starting-point. At the back of the book is a list of organisations which you may want to contact for further information.

*****

Making sense of censorship

Information from Family and Youth Concern

By Arthur Cornell

In November 2000, I attended the Channel 4 conference 'Making Sense of Censorship' at the Institute of Contemporary Arts in London. It was designed to bring together interested parties to discuss the revised guidelines for film classification produced by the British Board of Film Censorship (BBFC).

The background to the new guidelines, given in the paper produced by the chair of the BBFC, indicated that there had been wide-ranging consultation by a variety of means before the guidelines were finally drawn up. At the conference there were a number of discussion groups examining the implications of the results from various aspects. I was in the group entitled, Protecting the Innocent. Both the conference presentations and the smaller discussion groups raised a number of issues:

- the range of views came from across the whole spectrum, from those who wished to see all forms of censorship removed to those who recognised the need to protect the young and the vulnerable. Consensus is impossible because there are no accepted common values.
- discussion revealed the significance of semantics. The word 'adult' is used to describe those given access to films which many would question as being a reflection of a truly 'adult' mentality, while the word 'freedom' is used to mean 'to do as I like' rather than 'to become who I am'.
- the new guidelines have the problem of being all things to all people. This does mean that there will be very little, if any, constraints on films designed to be available only through sex shops (18R), but censors reviewing films in other categories will, now,

have to take account of scenes likely to provoke imitative behaviour.

The whole area of film censorship is overshadowed by the implications of what is available on the Internet, much of which is more disturbing than anything seen on films. This material can be accessed by individuals in a private context and is much more difficult to control than what is in the public arena in the film world. Consider the number

> **The whole area of film censorship is overshadowed by the implications of what is available on the Internet, much of which is more disturbing than anything seen on films**

of young people who now have a TV and/or a computer with Internet access in their own bedroom!

One of the most interesting features of the conference was the opportunity to meet university professors engaged in research into the effects of violence and pornography. There does appear to be significant evidence to show the effect of pornography on the treatment of women and the effects of violence on vulnerable adolescent male offenders. This does not surprise us but it is important to know that evidence is emerging. I understand that the Home Office has asked for research into whether it is possible to identify the 'vulnerable' before the stage of adolescence is reached. It would seem wise to 'watch this space' as the guidelines apply to films and videos, many of which will appear on our television screens.

• The above information is an extract from the bulletin produced by Family and Youth Concern. See page 41 for their address details.

© Family and Youth Concern

Film censor to stop playing nanny

The man who decides what's fit for us to see at the cinema is predicting an end to legally-enforced ratings

By Vanessa Thorpe, Arts Correspondent

Britain's most influential arbiter of public taste, the film censor, is predicting the end of legally enforced cinema ratings in the UK. In a speech on the future of censorship this week, Robin Duval will argue that greater freedom for filmmakers and audiences is on its way.

'We are pretty much the only country left to enforce a film rating system by law,' he said. 'In most of northern Europe and the Americas, film regulation is advisory and not mandatory. How long will Britain keep this up? As the internet and new media become more available, everyone wonders why one medium is regulated by law and another isn't.'

Duval, director of the British Board of Film Classification (BBFC) for just over two years, does not expect all forms of film classification to disappear. He envisages a grading scheme in which parents would be able to take children to see films they deem suitable. Existing legislation covering obscenity and child abuse would then become the only statutory public protection. In contrast, when the late Princess Diana controversially took an under-age Prince Harry to see the 15-certificate film *The Devil's Own* , the London cinema involved was threatened with prosecution under the 1985 Cinemas Act.

> **'We are pretty much the only country left to enforce a film rating system by law. In most of northern Europe and the Americas, film regulation is advisory and not mandatory'**

'I suspect film producers will still want their product to be given some sort of bill of health,' said Duval, 'but I think the legal nature of it will change fairly soon. Television will have to have its own ratings system too.'

Duval will use his speech at the Royal Society of Arts on Wednesday to call on the Government to rethink its policy on monitoring broadcast standards. New Labour plans for one giant, over-arching watchdog to look after film, television and the internet are dangerous, he will argue, and are also based on false assumptions.

The Government's parliamentary consultation document on the communications industry, published at Christmas, outlined plans for a new body, dubbed OfCom, to take over the roles of the Independent Television Commission, the Broadcasting Standards Council, the Radio Authority, the Radio Communications Agency and Oftel.

Duval said: 'There would be too much power in one institution – a supreme cultural regulator. Video and film would be lost within the broadcast bias of this watchdog.'

OfCom has been billed by the Government as a simplification of conflicting standards as the worlds of new media and broadcasting converge. But Duval and his

colleagues at the BBFC, including the president, Andreas Whittam Smith, are not convinced by the argument that filmed entertainment will all soon be delivered via the internet. 'There are a lot of assumptions being made that people will gravitate towards their homes,' said Duval. 'It is doubtful whether the expectation of this great convergence is justified.

'People want to have somewhere to go in the evening. There are actually now three times more people going to the cinema than in the middle of the 1980s.' Duval believes it will take a long time for the internet to become a central part of the film business. Sport is still the driving force behind home satellite and digital ownership and no film channel yet receives more than 1 per cent of viewing figures.

Attitudes to sex on screen have been deliberately relaxed since Duval and Whittam Smith have been in charge at the BBFC. 'We carried out research into public attitudes last year and there was a clear message,' said Duval. 'People believed the BBFC was being quite unnecessarily nannyish when it came to questions of sex, but attitudes to violence were less tolerant.' The BBFC's rating categories would continue to be rigorous over violence. Duval said that although the link between people seeing violence on screen and committing it was poor, the BBFC had to respond to public feeling.

Public acceptability is one of the BBFC's main criteria for rating films. 'The only statutory restriction we have is on violence towards animals under the 1937 Animals Act. We also have some restrictions under the Obscene Publications Act,' said Duval.

The BBFC ensures there is no mention of drugs in U-rated films. Even at PG level, however, there is more scope for referring to illicit substances, while at a 12-rating Duval says audiences are allowed to 'enter the real world', as long as there is no appearance of promoting drugs. 'Broadly, we have to steer away from "imitable techniques". And we will not allow any detail of a hanging in a 15-film,' he said.

Duval believes he has seen the

> *People believed the BBFC was being quite unnecessarily nannyish when it came to questions of sex, but attitudes to violence were less tolerant*

end of the recent tide of violent horror films. However, he is concerned that the industry is about to erupt into a spate of brutal adventure movies.

In contrast to current British concerns, American censorship has been tougher on sex than violence. In 1929 the Hays Office Code ruled that married couples had to be shown in twin beds and that one foot must stay on the floor in love scenes, lest the nation's collective morals were damaged.

• The above article first appeared in *The Observer*.
© *Guardian Newspapers Limited 2001*

Classification guidelines

Information from the British Board of Film Classification

i. There are seven classification categories
U, Uc and PG which are advisory only
12, 15 and 18 which restrict viewing by age
R18 which is only available to adults in licensed outlets

ii. Occasionally, a work lies on the margin between the two categories. In making a final judgement, the BBFC takes into account the intentions of the film-maker, the expectations of the public in general and the work's audience in particular, and any special merits of the work.

iii. Classification decisions may be stricter on video than on film. This is because of the increased possibility of under-age viewing recognised in the Video Recordings Act, and of works being replayed or viewed out of context. Accordingly, a work may receive a higher age classification on video, or require heavier cuts.

iv. Classification decisions are most strict on trailers and advertisements. This is because difficult content, which may be mediated by the context of the original work, may have a much starker effect in the brief and unprepared context of the trailer/advertisement.

v. Classification decisions may be less strict where they are justified by context.

vi. Anything not permitted in these Guidelines at a particular category (PG to 18) is unacceptable also at all preceding lower categories. Similarly, anything permitted at one level is acceptable at all higher levels.

• The above information is an extract from the web site of the British Board of Film Classification (BBFC), see www.bbfc.org.uk
© *British Board of Film Classification (BBFC)*

What should 12-year-olds be trusted to see?

'It is difficult to write a rule which ensures that under-12s will be accompanied by a parent or responsible adult.' By Andreas Whittam Smith

Should the '12' certificate in the cinema become advisory? This would mean that parents would decide whether children below the age of 12 would be able to attend films classified for the 12-to-14 age group. At present, the rating is mandatory. Under-12s are not supposed to go to '12' movies even if accompanied by their mother, their father, their grandparents and the local priest.

I write 'not supposed' because a certain amount of dodging goes on. Friends have told me how they took, say, 11-year-old Sophie or Euan to see *The Mummy* despite its '12' rating and have dared me to disapprove. I don't cluck my tongue because, frankly, the '12' rating does have problems. The maturity of children at around that age varies widely and parents are the best judges of their robustness. And cinema staff, too, cannot necessarily distinguish between an 11-year-old, for instance, and a 13-year-old, just by looking.

Moreover, the '12' rating is still highly restrictive. *Billy Elliot*, in many ways a natural '12', was classified at '15' because of the extensive use of four-letter words, albeit in a conversational rather than aggressive manner. The rule at '12' is that strong language should be rare and justified by context. As to violence, there should be no dwelling on detail and no emphasis on blood and injuries. Sexual violence can only be implied or briefly indicated and in any case without physical detail. Likewise, sexual activity may only be implied. Sexual references must do no more than reflect standards set by sex education in schools. There can be horror movies at '12' but limited to occasional gory moments. Similarly, references to soft drugs or scenes where soft drugs are used must be brief and few in number. They must

be justified by context and indicate the dangers. Hard drugs are off limits.

> *Under-12s are not supposed to go to '12' movies even if accompanied by their mother, their father, their grandparents and the local priest*

Crouching Tiger, Hidden Dragon was classified at '12' because the considerable violence was cast in the form of stylised martial arts. It is always a consideration to what extent form distances violence from the viewer. To take a different example, the excellent Australian film, *The Dish*, seemed to me to be a sort of modern miracle because of the almost complete absence of sex and violence. The 'dish' refers to an Australian radio telescope which found itself playing an important role in the American moon landing.

Here, the decision went the other way. *The Dish* would have been a PG (parental guidance) except for one bit of bad language; this raised it to the '12' category. Another example of a '12' is *Pearl Harbor*, which seems to be as big a commercial disaster for the makers as the actual event was for the American navy. *The Mummy Returns*, now for me indelibly associated with Lady Thatcher ever since her ponderous reference to it, is also, like its predecessor, a '12'.

As it happens, a good illustration of the difficulties of the mandatory '12' is coming up. *Lara Croft Tomb Raider*, rated '12', will open shortly. This is a big-budget film version of a successful computer game. It is a story of a quest for a magic device which gives the possessor the power to control time. The acrobatic, all-guns-blazing Lara fights an evil society – as well as passing robots – for its possession.

Large numbers of youngsters, whether or not they have quite reached their 12th birthdays, will want to go to it for they have already seen the Lara Croft character on computer screens. As a matter of fact, though, the version submitted to the British Board of Film Classification did conflict with the rule that 'realistic and contemporary weapons should not be glamorised'. The main problem concerned shots emphasising the attractiveness of flick knives. The film company took the board's concerns seriously and brought the movie into line with the '12' guidelines.

There are, however, major problems confronting any plan to make the '12' certificate advisory. One is the issue of accompaniment. It is difficult to write a rule which ensures that under-12s will be accompanied by a parent or responsible adult. At the box office window, the cinema staff have no way of ascertaining whether the older person who presents him or herself is indeed the parent or nominated by the parent. Insisting on adult accompaniment might encourage some kids to ask complete strangers to take them into desired movies.

When older readers of this newspaper were young teenagers, using a willing stranger to get one into a forbidden film was a recognised practice and I don't remember any reports of harmful experiences. But those days of innocence have passed. Paedophiles might see an opportunity. Is there any way of designing a satisfactory accompaniment requirement?

Another issue is consumer information. If parents are to decide whether to let younger children go to a '12' rated movie, they need to know what sort of film it is. The board provides consumer advice on its website (www.bbfc.co.uk) for every film and video passed. But the board has no power to insist that the film and video industry uses it in its advertising. Until now, the cinema distributors and owners have been unenthusiastic.

A further question is the manner in which the board should proceed in exploring the case for a change. The frame within which the board operates is the law. In the cinema,

the most relevant statutes are The Protection of Children Act 1978, The Obscene Publications Act 1959, the 1937 act which makes it illegal to show any scene involving actual cruelty to animals and the new legislation on human rights.

If parents are to decide whether to let younger children go to a '12' rated movie, they need to know what sort of film it is

---

Within these bounds, the board sites its detailed guidelines and these govern individual classification decisions. The important point is that the board's guidelines are designed to reflect public opinion as closely as possible. In a sense, the board has no view of its own. It does what it believes the public, particularly parents, wish it to do. In turn, cinema owners can operate only if they have a licence from the local authority, an invariable condition of which is that the board categories be observed unless the authority makes an exception for a specific film.

How, then, to test the proposition that '12' should become advisory rather than mandatory? I think the question must be put in the following form: would parents approve a relaxation in the rules provided that useful consumer information about individual '12' category films was readily available? Of course, this begs the further question whether better information can be provided. To this end, the co-operation of the cinema owners and distributors and involvement of local authorities will be essential.

There are signs that this can be secured. And once the board can put the question in a form which ties in better consumer information, then the methods used to test public opinion can be used again. It may also be possible to organise an experiment, perhaps lasting three to six months, in a single local authority area. The bottom line, however, is that the board will not make a permanent change unless satisfied the public approves. Public opinion will have the decisive say.

• The writer is the president of the British Board of Film Classification.

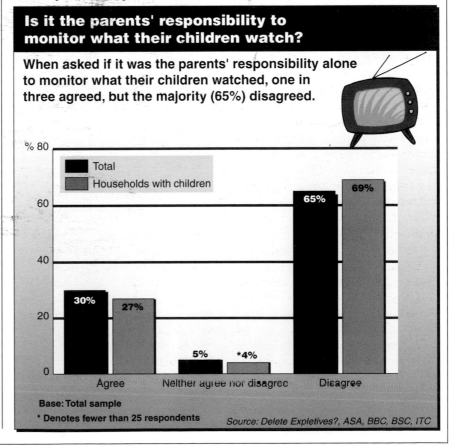

Is it the parents' responsibility to monitor what their children watch?

When asked if it was the parents' responsibility alone to monitor what their children watched, one in three agreed, but the majority (65%) disagreed.

Base: Total sample
* Denotes fewer than 25 respondents

Source: Delete Expletives?, ASA, BBC, BSC, ITC

Campaign against censorship

Film and video censorship

The Campaign's position is as follows:

1. All films should be released uncut.
2. There should be no power to ban films.
3. Certificates should be issued, but only as a guide for consumers.
4. Parents are responsible for what their children see on the screen. Adults are responsible for themselves.
5. There is no cause-and-effect connection between antisocial behaviour on the screen and antisocial behaviour in real life.

Some reasons for the position (not necessarily in order of importance and not necessarily all supported by all members of CAC):

1. A film is a work of art. It should be shown as its creator intended it to be. Cutting a film is the same as mutilating a painting or a statue; it is vandalism.

Films are cut for the cinema for purely commercial reasons. The largest market for cinema is the 14-17 age group. If a film is given a 15 certificate, it stands a better chance of making money than if it gets an 18. Cuts are agreed between the British Board of Film Classification and the distributor. For cinema film the BBFC is appointed by and responsible to the film industry. (For video it is responsible to the Home Office.)

Feature films on commercial television may be cut just to fit them between the ad breaks.

2. A list of films which were refused a certificate by the BBFC includes some of the greatest classics. Today, the decision to ban them looks ridiculous.

People ask for films to be banned because they frighten them. It is wrong to stop somebody else watching a film because it frightens you.

It is not the business of the state to control what people think. It is in any case impossible, even under the grossest dictatorship, to stop people thinking differently from those in charge.

There is no such thing as a snuff movie. (Defined as film of real murders sold as entertainment.) All such films turn out, when examined frame by frame, to be more or less simulated. Making film of real-life criminal acts is not more criminal than the acts themselves.

There is not a vast market for films dealing in very deviant sexual behaviour. By definition, the more deviant the behaviour, the fewer people are interested in it. Ordinary people will not become interested in it just because it is available. It is not the business of the law to prevent members of any minority group exchanging material provided the making of it does not involve real injury to real people without their consent.

3. The BBFC is fully aware that if a film is certified 18 some 17- and 16-year-olds will get to see it, and if it is a 15 some 14- and 13-year-olds will. They issue certificates with that in mind.

It should be the cinema managers' decision who they admit to the cinema, and the video dealers' decision who they sell or rent to.

There should be a system of certificates as a rough guide to the content of a film. Some people, adults as well as children, are more easily shocked or frightened than others and should be helped to avoid what will distress them. There is not and cannot be any guarantee that a scene in a 15 or 12 certificate film will not upset an adult by touching on their personal anxiety or fear, or that a scene in a PG or a U will not do the same for a child. But that is the fault of the experience which gave them that fear, not of the film.

4. The fact that some parents cannot or will not be responsible for the welfare of their children does not mean that all parents should be

treated as though they were irresponsible. Most parents are responsible; they know something about the way their children's minds work and they take trouble to inform themselves about the content of the films they propose to see. Children whose parents cannot or will not look after them have problems which banning every 18 certificate film ever made will not solve.

Cutting or banning a film intended for adults is treating adults like children. Nobody has the right to say to another child 'I know better than you what you should see.' To keep an adult in a state of childishness by preventing them making their own choices is wrong.

Over two-thirds of households in this country contain nobody under sixteen. Nothing should be banned merely because it might be taken into one of the other third.

Videos do not walk into houses by themselves.

5. Normal people over the age of about eight know the difference between the imaginary and the real. Anybody else who claims that a work of fiction has influenced them to the point of action in real life is either mentally handicapped, mentally ill or lying. Anybody who makes that claim on their behalf is either grinding their own axe, getting paid for it, or both.

To ban a film because it might encourage, or might have encouraged, a mentally-ill person to do something is to treat the entire population as though they were sick. If somebody behaves dangerously after seeing a film it can never be said that they would not have behaved like that without it. People choose films because of the way they already think and feel. You don't go to the cinema or get out a video if you're not in the mood for it.

All studies purporting to show a cause-and-effect connection are invalid:
a) For the 'mood' reason just given.
b) Because no reputable scientist claims that the way subjects behave under test conditions is the same as the way they behave

in their normal environment.
c) Because all studies based on self-selected samples (such as convicted offenders or student volunteers) are distorted. People take part in them because they have something to gain by doing so, even if it's only the amusement of filling in a questionnaire.
d) Because people are not as stupid as the researchers think. As soon as the questions are asked, they know what answers are being looked for.
e) Because, nearly always, people who go looking for a cause-and-effect connection believe that it is there. This belief influences the questions they ask and the results they get. Many studies are commissioned by pro-censorship campaigners. When looking at 'research' always notice who paid for it.

The above applies equally to cinema film, video, and feature films shown on television. A film does not become something different because it is being fed through a different machine.

All video recorders and TV sets have a switch called 'off'.

On TV censorship, and specifically the 9 pm 'watershed':
1. It is parents' responsibility to supervise what their children watch. The fact that some parents are irresponsible does not justify behaving as though they all were.
2. To suggest, as pro-censorship groups do, that because some

children are watching TV at all hours of the day and night, TV at all hours of the day and night should be suitable for children to watch, is to encourage irresponsible 'dump the kids in front of the telly' parenting.
3. Children of school age should not be watching TV late at night no matter what is on. They should be in bed.
4. In other European countries, the 'watershed' is later, but after it anything goes. This reflects i) a different attitude to family life and ii) a different attitude to what is shown.
5. The alleged welfare of children should not be used as an excuse to censor material intended for adults. Would-be censors are very fond of exploiting people's fears about what goes into children's heads.
6. Two-thirds of UK households contain nobody under sixteen.
7. The Campaign believes that all feature films shown on TV should be shown as they were made for the cinema – unexpurgated and uncut.

Campaign Against Censorship statement of aims

The guiding principles of the campaign are:
1. The right to obtain and impart knowledge.
2. Freedom from censorship.
3. Freedom for creative artists to present their perceptions, interpretations and ideas.
4. Support for victims of censorship without discrimination on the grounds of sex, sexual orientation, race, politics or religion.

'Everyone has the right to freedom of opinion and expression; this right includes freedom to hold opinions without interference and to seek, receive and impart information and ideas through any media and regardless of frontiers.'
– Universal Declaration of Human Rights (Article 19)

• The above information is an extract from a briefing sheet produced by the Campaign Against Censorship. See page 41 for their address details.
© Campaign Against Censorship

The scary truth about horror movies

. . . they're not. By Barbara Ellen, *The Observer*

If, as the pro-censorship lobby claims, people really do get homicidal ideas from movies, there must be some lame psychopaths around these days. To illustrate: the other evening, I had the opportunity to go and see *Hannibal*, the record-breaking sequel to *Silence of the Lambs*, starring Anthony Hopkins as the charismatic foppish cannibal Hannibal Lecter. Instead, I opted to stay in, flop on my bed, and watch the television airing of *Manhunter*, Michael Mann's lesser-known prequel to *Silence of the Lambs*.

Why? Because I'd seen *Manhunter*, and I knew it was sincerely horrifying. By contrast, I had become slightly fatigued by the media circus around Hannibal The Cannibal — the overblown poster campaign, endless newspaper epistles, and avalanche of television tie-ins about real-life cannibalism. As a friend commented, the *Hannibal* hype-athon was like another round of those ghastly 'foodie' programmes, only this time they were eating people. Besides, I'm choosy about what I'd call frightening, and for all that, *Hannibal* looked fun in its own way — it also looked set to be about as genuinely scary as a trip to an out-of-season pantomime.

Sorry to be a killjoy (boom, boom), but it seems pertinent to address the fact that the 'scariest movie of the year' doesn't look scary at all in the week that moves were made to end the legally enforced cinema ratings system in this country. This means that adult Britons will finally be allowed to practise self-censorship — deciding for themselves whether a movie is beyond the pale or actually far less shocking than the price of popcorn. The good news is that, if these changes go through, everything we see or don't see will be up to us. Trouble is, without the censors to act like scissor-happy

nannies on our behalf, it looks like we're going to have a very hard time finding anything to get shocked about.

The likes of Mary Whitehouse have always been deemed to be the bane of popular culture, but without their kneejerk squawks of protest, the big-girl's-blouse of modern cinema would be lost. For, when you think about, it has been some time since a horror movie really shook one to the core in the way that, say, *The Exorcist* or *The Texas Chain Saw Massacre* did in the 70s, or *Henry: Portrait of a Serial Killer* did in the 80s. It says something that the closest the 90s got to hardcore horror was a bunch of students running about in the woods screaming at each other's terrible dress sense in *The Blair Witch Project*. The rest was all Dame Freddie, the *Scream* irony-athons. Or that kid from *The Sixth Sense*, who was supposed to be psychic but failed to spot that co-star Bruce Willis's career had been dead for some time.

Then, of course, there was *Silence of the Lambs*. A good movie, yes, an entertaining movie, sure, but scary? Hardly. Talking as somebody who, in terms of adolescent sensationalism, was suckled at the tit of Stephen King and *Hammer House of Horror*, *Silence of the Lambs* seemed about as frightening as a rubber bat dangling off a stick. Indeed, anybody who had enjoyed Thomas Harris's books could only have been alarmed at how suddenly camp and cuddly the screen Lecter had become.

When Brian Cox took on the same role in *Manhunter*, he did so with dry, succinct malevolence. Good man. Good actor. Then Hopkins arrived, overacting like some fruity provincial clergyman. 'Look,' I screamed disgustedly at anyone who would listen. 'He's turned Lecter into a girl.' Watching the movie again recently, and shuddering afresh at all the leaden flirting between Hopkins and Jodie Foster, I realised that the situation was worse than that. Hopkins, Harris and the multi-billion-dollar industry that is Lecter Inc seem hellbent on turning Hannibal into some kind of charismatic, lovable flesh-eating psychopath. Give or take a few anti-social habits, Hannibal Lecter was more or less James Bond. Which is all very well, until we are made to suffer big windy articles about how depraved society has become to accept a dreadful cinema baddie like Hannibal Lecter. How irredeemably wussy have we become as a global audience if a cannibal — who only eats when he's hungry, and then with cloth napkins — is deemed to be as bad as it gets. Lecter is less frightening than he should be, having long sacrificed his vérité bite at the altar of meretricious, crowd-pleasing foppery. All *Hannibal* proves is that, just as most people will laugh at anything if it is signposted well enough, they will scream at pretty much anything too. Anyone who disagrees can just bite me.

© Guardian Newspapers Limited 2001

Can the net stay free?

This house believes that any attempt by government to police the internet is both unworkable and a severe threat to civil liberties. This motion will be debated at the Oxford Union by David Kerr (against) and Yaman Akdeniz (for).

The case against

This motion addresses fundamental issues for the future of the internet in the UK, and worldwide. The Internet Watch Foundation is at the heart of the debate as it was set up by internet service providers to help police criminal content, primarily child pornography, and avoid a severe threat to civil liberties.

Based on experience in IWF and elsewhere, there are demonstrably some workable means for government to police the internet. But the means are very different from traditional approaches to older media. They need to be through partnership and co-regulation with industry rather than authoritarian enforcement.

The UK government and law enforcement were perhaps the first to realise that they would best achieve their objectives by working with the ISP (internet service provider) industry rather than against it. There is now a familiar pattern of public reporting of suspect content through a hotline, followed by a notice and take down procedures to remove content assessed as illegal by the hotline. It has been taken up in similar forms by half-a-dozen other European countries, in the USA and most recently in Australia.

Similar co-regulatory solutions seem to emerge on the heels of other problems. Labelling and filtering addresses the threats of content potentially harmful to children. E-commerce will pose big problems, but the size and economics of the market make willing bedfellows of government, industry and law enforcement to provide safe trading.

Thus workable means for governments to police emerging problems on the net are already in place. I would stress workable: they are not perfect, just as policing off-line is far from perfect.

In each of the emerging mea-sures, governments are being obliged to rely on co-regulatory modes of operation. The net's architecture itself allows individual users of the internet to keep control of their choices about how they use it.

Most people have an offshore option to avoid unreasonable re-straints. So government policing in the workable forms I advocate poses little threat to fundamental civil liberties.

> *The net's architecture itself allows individual users of the internet to keep control of their choices about how they use it*

In my view, the greatest danger to civil liberties arises if governments do not learn how to achieve adequate regulation by new means and are panicked into imposing authoritarian measures, even if that means throw-ing the baby out with the bath water.

Thus my conclusion contradicts the motion: there is a severe threat to civil liberties if governments do not find workable ways to police the internet.

David Kerr, Chief Executive, Internet Watch Foundation.

The case for

The internet, as a global medium, is thought to be the land of free speech and democracy. However, we are at a time when censorship of the internet is increasing in the UK. Internet content is facing censorship from public bodies, the service providers and private regulatory bodies such as the Internet Watch Foundation.

Following the judgment in the Demon case, the ISPs have been pressured to take down internet content for allegedly carrying defamatory content under the Defamation Act 1996.

For example, the website of Jim Hulbert, which was critical of some judges and the Lord Chancellor's department, was taken down in November 1999 following a 'notice' being sent to a Hull-based ISP.

Regulate the Internet?

Most respondents (whether or not they have access to the Internet) think the medium should be regulated, although substantial percentages feel this would be impossible.

	With Internet access %	Without Internet access %
Internet should be regulated	41	39
Internet should be regulated/ but not possible	39	25
Internet should not be regulated	13	5
Don't know	8	30

Source: Concerning Regulation, Broadcasting Standards Commission

largely left to private enterprise. Schools or education authorities have been able to make their own arrangements, or pick from a number of government-approved suppliers. Household names such as Apple, IBM and Bull have been quick to jump into the market, and it is certainly true that the UK education system is now among the most connected in the world. The crucial question is: connected to what?

Following Blunkett's instructions, each supplier is obliged to filter all communications to and from the Internet. Special software is used, either on the desktop or more commonly at server level – i.e., at the point of contact to the Internet proper – to monitor student traffic. Certain page requests will be denied, certain downloaded files will be confiscated, certain conversations will be terminated. Even Apple, famed for their 'Think Different' advertising campaign, knuckled under; their National Grid for Learning services page is headed: 'Secure, fast and filtered'. If the software removed all pornography, or information about home-made drugs or firearms, or censored anything else that even anti-censorship campaigners would not want a five-year-old puzzling over and *cut nothing else*, then perhaps we could rest easy. But it does far more.

An example: Bull uses Symantec's I-Gear to filter UK schools access. The software is reckoned to be state of the art: the experience of students in New York suggests otherwise. In autumn 1999, I-Gear began filtering the Board of Education's access. Jan Shakofsky, a humanities teacher at Benjamin Cardozo High School, is reported in the *New York Times* as saying that her students hit the filter whenever they tried to 'research the pros and cons of an issue'. For instance, when looking at gun control they found the National Rifle Association's site was blocked. Similarly, 'Access denied' greeted attempts to research bulimia, child labour, AIDS – even a chapter of John Steinbeck's *Grapes of Wrath* was off limits, because of a passage where a starving man suckles at a mother's breast. When it

encounters an unfamiliar site, I-Gear uses the tried, if not to be trusted, method of filtering based on a set of prohibited words. However, the software can also check its internal file of blocked sites, regularly updated by Symantec's head office. In fact, left to its default settings I-Gear 'disappears' thousands of websites that find their way on to Symantec's 23 category, hand-compiled list. Whose hand?

Meet Michael Cherry – Michael's a hard-working guy. As systems administrator for Hory County schools, South Carolina, Michael keeps track of every Web page request made by students at local schools, sometimes live, sometimes after the event, perusing printouts of access requests. His schools use I-Gear, but Michael knows Hory County: 'We're deep in the Bible Belt' he says. He keeps an eye out for any offensive material that slips through the filters, and when he finds such a site, he tells Symantec. Symantec listens, and lists . . .

Many censorware programs intentionally block non-pornographic dissenting or fringe content in areas such as drug abuse and race issues

---

Norman Siegel of the New York Civil Liberties Union remarked of I-Gear: 'The blocking program sweeps far too broadly. It significantly undermines teachers' ability to conduct their lessons and students' ability to complete their classroom assignments.'

Back in the UK, another best-selling filter program, CyberPatrol, is the choice of another government-approved supplier, Centerprise. CyberPatrol was one of the first 'censorware' programs, and in the last few years has been found to block the MIT Student Association for Freedom of Expression, Planned Parenthood, the Ontario Centre for Religious Tolerance, the 'Why AOL Sucks' website, the HIV/AIDS

Information Center of the Journal of the American Medical Association, the alt.atheism and soc.feminism newsgroups and many more entirely legitimate and non-pornographic sites. This despite CyberPatrol's claims that they evaluate all sites manually. It also has a nasty habit of blocking sites that criticise it or its filtering techniques, or that suggest ways in which students can evade or disable its software.

British astronomer Heather Couper tells the story of a boy complaining to her that he cannot access a website she has co-developed – the filtering software in his school blocks it. Why? Because the site deals with back-garden 'naked eye observations'.

What is clear to anyone with knowledge of filtering software is that any automatic blocking of porn or violence is accompanied by a massive unintentional blocking of innocent and potentially useful sites. In addition, many censorware programs intentionally block non-pornographic dissenting or fringe content in areas such as drug abuse and race issues. Such heavy-handed gagging, if discovered, can only cause harm: does David Blunkett really believe a student will place *more* trust in a teacher's word if all dissenting voices are erased?

Filtering aside, Blunkett's 'Superhighway Safety Pack' also makes clear that material intended for educational purposes has to pass a number of tests before it can be considered suitable for inclusion on the National Grid for Learning web site. In fact, the NGfL will not even link to sites unless they abide by strict rules and, again, do not contain 'unsuitable' material. But it doesn't end there. If you want to provide an educational resource online, you not only have to ensure your own site is squeaky clean, you must also ensure that you don't link to any other sites that might contain unsuitable material. Are we still talking pornography? Unfortunately not.

I asked a DfEE spokesman for clarification on exactly what material was considered 'unsuitable' for inclusion on, or linking to, that NGfL site. He was unable to come up with examples so I ran through some of the material *Index on Censorship* currently holds on its website. Linking to mirrors of *Green Anarchist* magazine would not be acceptable – the word 'anarchist' was enough to convince the DfEE that our children would not benefit from reading it. More shocking was the DfEE's reaction to Nadire Mater's ground-breaking article presenting the voices of Turkey's conscript soldiers. Her recording of tales of bullying, drug abuse, murder and atrocity has left Mater facing up to five years' jail for 'defaming the Turkish army' – free speech is not highly regarded in Turkey (*Index* 5/1999). Nor it seems in the UK. British teenagers could not be allowed to read of the brutalising treatment handed out to conscripted Turkish teenagers, nor the mutilations they in turn handed on to Kurds. Why? Perhaps because if they did they might ask why the UK sold arms to Turkey? Perhaps because they might wonder why a NATO army could carry out atrocities against Kurds while bombing others for the same crimes against Kosovars?

It might seem that provocative materials drawing on real-life situations that students see on TV would form a strong basis for classroom discussion, that in Labour's much vaunted 'Citizenship' classes the analysis of democratic values would be enhanced by looking at the limits of tolerance, the boundaries placed on dissent here and abroad.

At times that is the message we hear from government. The reality is very different. Twelve million of our fellow citizens are having to get used to the idea that what they read, what they say, who they talk to is controlled not by their parents or their teachers, but at best by a faceless bureaucrat in Whitehall, at worst by a dull little sub-routine on a UNIX server, humming away in the corner of an anonymous business unit somewhere in our grey unpleasant land.

• The above information is an extract from *Index on Censorship*, the magazine produced by Index on Censorship. See page 41 for their address details.

© *Index on Censorship*

Web inventor denounces net censorship

By John Arlidge, Media Correspondent

On the tenth anniversary of the creation of the internet, the British scientist who invented the world wide web has called for the abolition of censorship online. As parents' groups and politicians press for new ways to police websites, Tim Berners-Lee rejects censorship as 'horrific'.

In an exclusive interview with *The Observer* , Berners-Lee dismisses the recent outcry over paedophiles targeting youngsters in web chat-rooms, child pornography and fraud, and rejects calls for a 'net regulator'. 'I know there are some very strong feelings but you cannot banish technology or regulate content.

'Regulation is censorship – one grown-up telling another what they can and cannot do or see. For me, the idea is horrific. Universality is the key. You must be able to represent anything on the web.'

Illegal material – child pornography, 'video nasties' – should remain illegal, but he insists 'the world is a diverse place and we should trust people, not try to police them . . . There are many cultures and they are continually changing. What somebody in Tennessee might think of as reasonable when it comes to nudity is very different from what someone in Finland might think.

'Two neighbours next door to each other might have very different ideas. So any attempt to make a global centralised standard is going to be unbelievably contentious. You can't do that.' Instead of regulation it is up to parents to 'catch up' with the new e-generation and teach youngsters how to use the web safely. Children are at risk because they are 'tech-nologically ahead of most grown-ups, who have to ask the younger generation how to turn the thing on and get it working. Adults are slower than children. They need to catch up so they can teach their children what to see and what to avoid.'

Ten years ago Berners-Lee wrote the electronic code that enables computers across the world to 'talk' to each other down a telephone line. The internet was born and has grown from a single website to more than 800,000,000, with e-commerce, chatrooms and email transforming the way we work, shop, do business, socialise and relax.

The Manchester-born scientist has been hailed as 'the man who invented the future'. A decade on he says we are still 'just scratching the surface' of what the internet can do. 'The web is far from done. Just imagine you were back in the Middle Ages and somebody asked "Given the full impact that paper is going to have, where will we be?" That's where we are.'

He describes the future as 'the semantic web . . . a new, more powerful interactive network that will really enable e-commerce and industry to hum. But I don't want to say more or everyone will jump on the bandwagon and that will wreck it.'

He says his creation is 'progressing remarkably well . . . it's neat. It is an achievement of a group of people who had a twinkle in their eye about a possible future. We should celebrate the fact that we can change the world by creating a new social tool. It gives a great feeling of hope that we can do it again.'

• The above article first appeared in *The Observer*.

© *Guardian Newspapers Limited 2000*

New age rating symbols for computer games

Six-year analysis shows that most computer games are 'nice not nasty'

Parents and others who are concerned about the suitability of certain computer and video games for young children, and who are often confused by marketing hype and the technical jargon of gaming enthusiasts, will welcome the leisure software industry's introduction of new, clearer, on-pack age rating symbols. The symbols will start to appear on new releases as they arrive in stores in the pre-Christmas sales period.

The introduction of the new symbols coincides with the launch of statistics that show that, contrary to popular belief, the majority of computer games products published in the UK are not overtly violent or sexual in content and are in fact suitable for ages three upwards. Only 0.43% of games rated during the last six years under the industry's Voluntary Age Suitability Ratings system require an 18-plus age rating.

The new age rating symbols have been introduced by the European Leisure Software Publishers' Association (ELSPA) who, with the Video Standards Council (VSC), regulate the industry's voluntary age rating code of practice. They replace previous symbols, which were first introduced in 1994. The symbols indicate the suitability for certain age groups of a product's content in terms of depictions of violence, sex, criminal activity or language. The ratings do not relate to the degree of difficulty to play the game.

As part of the industry's endorsement of the code, the new symbols will be displayed more prominently on packs and ELSPA is encouraging publishers to show them on the front as well as the back of a pack.

Explaining the reasoning behind the new symbols, Roger Bennett, Director General of ELSPA, said: 'There is, quite rightly, concern among most of the public that children should not be exposed to graphic depictions of violence, sex, strong language or other adult activities whether these be in films, on television, computer games or in real life. At the same time, there is an equally valid concern that older members of the public should have the freedom to choose to watch adult material within common bounds of decency. Playing computer and video games is now a mainstream form of entertainment not just for children but for all ages, particularly the twenty and thirty-somethings. The range of titles available reflects the huge diversity of ages and tastes among the buying public.'

He added: 'Computer games are top of the Christmas and birthday presents' wish list for most children and yet the purchasers, particularly parents and older relatives, are often out of touch with what's hot and what's not. Naturally, there is often concern among gift buyers that what their child is requesting may not actually be suitable for their age. Also the fact that games are multi-level makes it difficult for parents to sample a game in its entirety before buying.

'For these reasons it is important that there is a trusted, impartial recommendation as to the suitability of a game that parents can trust. That is the purpose of the Voluntary Age Suitability Rating scheme. The clarity of the new symbols makes the age suitability unequivocal and we think that, in the run-up to Christmas particularly, this will be welcomed by most harassed parents and other gift buyers.'

He added: 'The analysis of age rated products over the last six years undermines those critics who glibly state that computer games and other products produced by the leisure software industry encourage violence or contribute to lowering moral

standards. Not true. The vast majority of the products produced by our members provide family entertainment as well as education and reference materials.'

This year, for the first time, sales of leisure software in the UK will top the magic £1 billion mark. The contribution to the economy in terms of jobs and tax revenue is immense and growing. This month, the Government recognised the importance of computer games as aids to learning and ELSPA is assisting the Department of Education and Employment in its work in this area with games developers.

How does the Voluntary Age Suitability Rating Scheme work?

First introduced in 1994, the Voluntary Age Suitability Rating Scheme has been hugely successful. Membership of ELSPA is dependent on a publisher abiding by the voluntary code of practice. There are no examples of a rating being challenged by a member of the public. In instances where a publisher has not agreed with the initial rating given, there have been a number of appeals, which have found in favour of the VSC rating. In all instances,

the publisher has agreed with the outcome and has used the ELSPA/VSC rating on pack.

The VSC Voluntary Age Rating procedure starts by ascertaining whether a game requires legal classification by the British Board of Film Classification (BBFC). Products requiring submission to the BBFC for classification are those that depict scenes of human sexual activity, gross violence towards humans or animals or images likely to encourage the commission of offences.

Since the voluntary system started in 1994, 3932 products have been rated of which only 219 (5.5%) have required submission to the BBFC. Of those submitted to the BBFC, only 77, or less than 2% of all the games rated during the last 6 years, have been classified with a BBFC rating of 'Over 18'. A further 17 products (or 0.4%) which are exempt from legal classification by

the BBFC, were given a Voluntary Age Rating code of 18 plus during the period. Products which fall into this category are those depicting nudity, violence towards vulnerable women and children, ethnic stereotypes, use of drugs or domestic violence.

Of all 3932 games rated during the period 1994 to September 1999, the vast majority – 2621 (or 66%) – were rated as suitable for ages three upwards.

It is interesting to note that there is no upwards trend for 18 and over products. As at 30 September 1999, only 2 products have been given a Voluntary Age Rating of 18 plus and only 11 products have required submission to the BBFC for classification.

What is ELSPA ?

The European Leisure Software Publishers' Association (ELSPA) represents the interests of the UK leisure software industry. Its members include almost all the major UK publishers and distributors of leisure software (computer games, reference, education and other interactive, multimedia CD ROMS).

© The European Leisure Software Publishers' Association (ELSPA)

Game classifications

Information from the Video Standards Council

It is probably true that most parents of children and young teenagers have grown up in the video age and therefore have a reasonable understanding of the legal classification system and an ability to decide whether a particular video is suitable for their children. If all else fails a parent can always watch the video before making a decision.

This is not always the case when it comes to video and computer games where all too often the child is more adept at using the computer and the parent sometimes doesn't know how to access what their child is playing. As a result it is important that parents have something to guide

them when making a decision on whether a game is suitable for their children.

There are two systems for games that parents can rely on.

Under the law games are generally exempt from the legal classification system that applies to video. However, this exemption can be lost usually because the

game shows realistic scenes of gross violence or sexual activity. If this happens the game must be legally classified and will receive one or other of the classification certificates. Usually the game will receive an age-restricted classification (12, 15 or 18) which makes it illegal for a shopkeeper to supply the game to anyone below the specified age.

Accordingly parents have the comfort of knowing that games of a more extreme nature are dealt with by the law. There is nothing wrong with a game with an age-restricted classification. It simply means that the game is not suitable for young children and is suitable for a more mature audience.

Since 1993 about 5% of games have lost their general exemption and have been given legal classifications.

This leaves about 95% of games which are not covered by the law. In 1993 the VSC joined forces with the European Leisure Software Publishers' Association (ELSPA) which is the trade body representing the large majority of games publishers in the UK.

It was recognised that whilst the large majority of games were and would probably remain exempt this did not mean that all exempt games were suitable for children of all ages. As a result of consultation between the VSC, ELSPA and a number of outside bodies (including organisations concerned with family and child welfare) the voluntary system of age-rating for games exempt from legal classification was devised. The system belongs to ELSPA but is administered by the VSC as an independent third party not influenced by commercial considerations.

Under the voluntary system games are rated at one of four different levels – ages 3+, 11+, 15+ and 18+. The suitability-rating given is indicated on the packaging by the use of a logo using green ticks to indicate the ages for which the game is suitable and red crosses to indicate the ages for which the game is not suitable.

From the autumn of 1999 onwards redesigned and more easily understood logos started to be used on newly released games.

These voluntary age-suitability ratings enable parents to make an informed choice when buying a game for their children.

It should be noted that the ratings relate to the content of the game and not to how difficult the game is to play. A chess game would probably get four green ticks or a 3+ but would hardly be recommended for toddlers.

Since 1994 until the end of 1999 over 3,800 games have been rated under the voluntary system with 70.12% receiving a 3+, 20.47% an 11+, 8.95% a 15+ and only 0.46% an 18+. It was always unlikely that many games would receive an 18+ under the voluntary system as any game reaching this level would probably have already lost its exemption and have to be legally classified.

These figures dispel the myth that most games are of a violent nature. The truth is quite the reverse.

The VSC would welcome any comments concerning the voluntary ratings system.

• The above information is an extract from the Video Standards Council's web site which can be found at www.videostandards.org.uk

© Video Standards Council

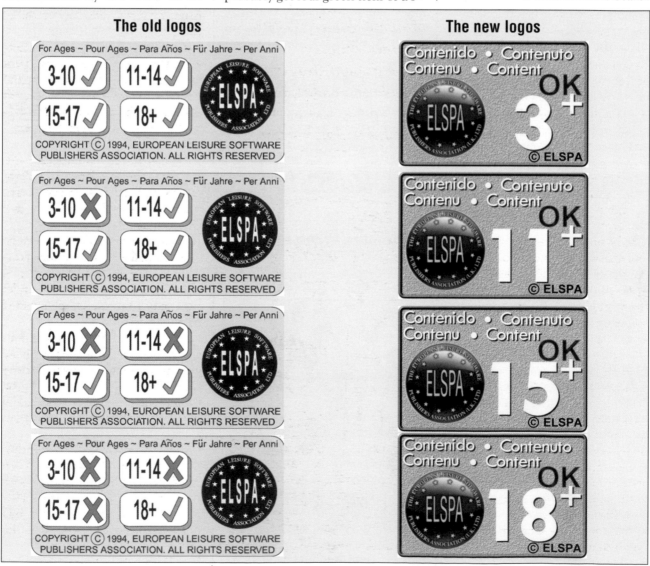

School massacre families to sue creators of violent games

The parents of children murdered during the Columbine High School shootings have launched a multibillion-dollar lawsuit against the makers of violent computer games, which they blame for having inspired the massacre.

The British computer games company Eidos has been named as a co-defendant in a $5bn (£3.6bn) lawsuit filed by parents of the Columbine victims, who were shot dead by two students who went on the rampage at the school near Denver, Colorado, in April 1999.

Eidos, which distributes the popular *Tomb Raider* game, has been named alongside companies that include ID Software, Paramount, Sega, Sony and Virgin Interactive, whose games are all alleged to have caused the shootings in which 15 people died.

Eric Harris and Dylan Klebold, the two students who launched the attack with semi-automatic weapons and pipe bombs, were among the dead.

The victims' parents allege that games such as Eidos's *Final Fantasy VII* led to the massacre, and say that the creators of those games 'knew or should have known that copycat violence would result from the use of their products and materials'. This case mirrors increasing concern in the United States over the violent content of films, television shows and computer games.

It is the second such case brought against computer games companies. In April last year, a judge dismissed a claim filed in Paducah, Kentucky, over another school shooting in December 1997 in which three people died. He ruled that the games companies 'owed no legal duty of care ...' because the killer's actions were 'unforeseeable', and also that to restrain the content of games would violate the United States' First Amendment, which guarantees freedom of speech.

By Charles Arthur, Technology Editor

The games most obviously on trial include two of the most popular 'shoot-'em-ups', namely *Doom* and *Quake*. In both, the players see themselves behind a gun or a rifle and attempt to kill their opponents. Other games under scrutiny include *Mortal Kombat*, *Redneck Revenge* and *Resident Evil*.

The victims' parents allege that games led to the massacre, and say that the creators of those games 'knew or should have known that copycat violence would result from the use of their products and materials'

One insider on the defendants' side said: 'The wording of the Columbine claim is virtually identical to the Paducah one.' He added: 'We think that will mean it will get thrown out in short order.'

Eidos has not set aside any funds against the possibility of losing the case, because it cannot quantify how much might be awarded if it lost.

The lawsuit could mark an important watershed in attitudes towards the increasingly violent computer games on sale in the United States.

During the American presidential debates last year, George Bush said: 'Columbine spoke to a larger issue, and it's really a matter of culture.

'It's a culture that somewhere along the line we begun to disrespect life, where a child can walk in and have their heart turn dark as a result of being on the internet, and walk in and decide to take somebody else's life.'

Jamie Love, an internet activist, said that the incidence of violent crimes had fallen in recent years, since games including *Doom* and *Quake* were released.

He said yesterday: '*Doom* was released in 1994. In the four years between the release of *Doom* and *Quake II*, the number of killers under the age of 18 in the US plummeted by 46 per cent.'

Eidos and the other games companies defending the lawsuit are waiting to hear when any trial might start. The writ was filed by the Columbine parents last month, and is likely to take some time to come to court.

A spokesman for Eidos said that the computer company had been named as a defendant in the Paducah case, but was released from that because the game in question had not even been released when the shooting in Kentucky happened.

Reflecting community values

Public attitudes to broadcasting regulation

Viewers want more respect for their interests, intelligence and privacy from broadcasters, according to a new study published by the Broadcasting Standards Commission today.

This is one of the key findings to emerge from an important piece of research undertaken by the Commission into the public's view towards broadcasting and its regulation. The study *Reflecting Community Values: Public Attitudes to Broadcasting Regulation* asked eight focus groups and a sample of 2008 respondents important questions such as:

- Given the rapid pace of technological change, should content regulation continue?
- If so, what should be its key features?
- What are the core values that broadcasters should respect?

Although participants in the research understood that digitalisation and converging communication markets brought increased choice, they were not convinced that more necessarily meant better. They regretted the loss of the common viewing experience and worried that as a result of the rapid technological changes around them, they have lost a sense of their own choice about what and how they view.

Lord Dubs of Battersea, Chairman of the Broadcasting Standards Commission, said: 'Broadcasters and regulators should ensure that the public do not feel undervalued and disempowered. They must find ways of including them in the new technological revolution that is taking place and involving them in the debate about the range of services on offer.'

The study shows that audiences still feel there is a need for regulation. They want broadcasters and regulators to continue:

- to offer the Watershed to protect children and vulnerable groups of society

- to show respect for their personal integrity, intelligence and privacy
- and to reflect Britain's community values.

However, there is an acknowledgement that regulation should work in conjunction with greater personal responsibility and parental choice, facilitated by appropriate information about the content of programmes.

Broadcasters and regulators should ensure that the public do not feel undervalued and disempowered

---

Community values were predominant in respondents' thinking about the core values that broadcasters should reflect. Whilst there was a wide variety of opinions, there

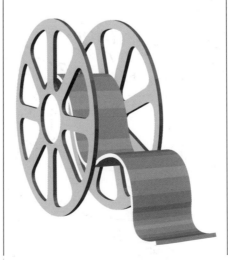

was a general consistency about the values which underlined them. Key amongst the personal values were reciprocity – 'do to others as you would have others do to you' – and honesty – 'be true to yourself'. Participants also highlighted the need to emphasise respect for suffering and grief.

Stephen Whittle, Director of the Broadcasting Standards Commission, said: 'We hope that the findings of this research will stimulate debate on matters of concern to citizens relating to regulation and community values.'

Notes
1. The Broadcasting Standards Commission is the statutory body for both standards and fairness in broadcasting. It is the only organisation within the regulatory framework of UK broadcasting to cover all television and radio, both terrestrial and satellite. This includes text, cable and digital services. It has three main tasks, as established by the 1996 Broadcasting Act. These are:
- to produce codes of conduct relating to standards and fairness;
- to consider and adjudicate on complaints; and
- to monitor, research and report on standards and fairness in broadcasting.

2. Copies of *Reflecting Community Values: Public Attitudes to Broadcasting Regulation*, Stefaan Verhulst, Programme in Comparative Media Law & Policy, Broadcasting Standards Commission are available at: www.bsc.org.uk

• The above information is an extract from the the Broadcasting Standards Commission's web site which can be found at www.bsc.co.uk Alternatively, see page 41 for their address details.
© *The Broadcasting Standards Commission*

The Broadcasting Standards Commission

The Broadcasting Standards Commission is the statutory body for both standards and fairness in broadcasting. It is the only organisation within the regulatory framework of UK broadcasting to cover all television and radio, both terrestrial and satellite. This includes text, cable and digital services. It has three main tasks, as established by the Broadcasting Act 1996. These are:

- to produce codes of conduct relating to standards and fairness;
- to consider and adjudicate on complaints;
- to monitor, research and report on standards and fairness in broadcasting.

Codes of guidance

The codes on standards and fairness give guidance on good practice which all broadcasters and their regulators are required to reflect. Research and consultation provide the basis for these guidelines.

Monitoring, researching and reporting

The Commission monitors the standards of UK and transfrontier broadcasting and, through a programme of independent research, reports on the attitudes of the public towards both standards and fairness issues. It may also report directly to the Secretary of State for Culture, Media and Sport on any issue arising from its work.

Complaints

The Commission considers two types of complaints: standards and fairness. It has the power to require recordings of broadcast material and written statements. It may also hold hearings. Its decisions are published regularly and broadcasters must report any action they have taken as a result. Additionally, the Commission can require broadcasters to publish summaries of its decisions on-air and in a newspaper or magazine.

Standards complaints

Anyone who has seen or heard a broadcast can make a complaint about the portrayal of violence, sex or other issues of taste and decency (such as bad language). In reaching its decision, the code and research are considered alongside the material and its context.

Fairness complaints

Only those people with a direct interest in a broadcast can complain of unfair treatment or unwarranted infringement of privacy. The Commissioners always study written exchanges of evidence and may hold a hearing with both the complainant and broadcaster present.

Accountability

The Commission is accountable to Parliament and each year publishes a full report of its work. It is financed by Government and broadcasters and its accounts are subject to scrutiny by the National Audit Office.

The Commission

Thirteen Commissioners are responsible for the work of the Commission, chaired by Lord Dubs of Battersea. All are appointed by the Secretary of State for Culture, Media and Sport and serve part-time for a period of three to five years. Their work is supported by a full-time staff managed by the Director, Paul Bolt.

- The above information is an extract from the Broadcasting Standards Commission's web site which can be found at www.bsc.co.uk

© The Broadcasting Standards Commission

The main concerns

Information from the British Board of Film Classification (BBFC)

Theme

The acceptability of a theme is determined by its treatment, i.e. the context and sensitivity of its presentation. However, the most problematic themes (for example drug abuse or paedophilia) are unlikely to be appropriate at the most junior levels of classification. Correspondingly, there is no reason in principle why any theme, however difficult, could not be satisfactorily handled at '18' or even '15'.

Language

Many people are offended, some of them deeply, by bad language, including the use of expletives with a religious association. The extent of that offence varies according to age, background and beliefs. Different groups (for example, a minority ethnic community) have their own, separate standards of acceptability. Additionally, the severity of any particular word or expression will depend upon the context within which it is used.

For these reasons, it is impossible to set out comprehensive lists of acceptable words or expressions which will satisfy all sections of the public. The advice at different classification levels, therefore, provides general guidance with reference to specific terms only where there is a reasonable consensus of opinion.

Nudity

Natural nudity, providing there is no sexual context or sub-text, is acceptable at all classification levels.

Sex

The portrayal of human sexual activity is not permitted at 'U', 'Uc' or 'PG'. In '12' rated works it may be implied only. Progressively more graphic portrayal may be included at

British Board of Film Classification

'15' and '18' depending on the emphasis given to responsible, loving and developing relationships. There is equality in terms of the standards set for legal heterosexual and homosexual behaviour. The 'R18' category, required by the Video Recordings Act, is primarily for explicit videos of consenting sex between adults. 'R18' videos may be supplied only in licensed sex shops which no one under 18 can enter.

Violence

Violence has been a feature of entertainment for children and adults since the first stories were told. It is an element in many serious representations of the human condition. We can, however, address the degree and nature of violence through our classification system. In making decisions, our concerns include:
- portrayal of violence as a normal solution to problems
- heroes who inflict pain and injury
- callousness towards victims
- encouraging aggressive attitudes
- taking pleasure in pain or humiliation

Works which glorify or glamorise violence will receive a more restrictive classification and may even be cut.

Attitudes

Emulation of violence

% agreeing (% disagreeing in brackets) %	National N=1249 %	Postal N=816 %	Internet N=1011 %	Juries Pre N=28 %	Juries Post N=27 %
Watching violence in films generally makes people more likely to be violent in real life	46 (28)	38 (41)	7 (85)	50 (25)	15 (70)

Over half the national sample (56%) agreed that young people might use bad language because of what they hear in films and videos. Just over a quarter of the sample disagreed. The postal sample was slightly less convinced (48% agreed, 34% disagreed) and most of the internet sample dismissed the idea out of hand (19% agreed, 64% disagreed, 37% strongly). Jurors, who were asked about the statement afterwards, demonstrated very little support for it (only one in ten agreeing).

Copying bad language

% agreeing (% disagreeing in brackets) %	National N=1249 %	Postal N=816 %	Internet N=1011 %	Juries Post N=27 %
Young people use bad language because of what they hear in films and videos	56 (26)	48 (34)	19 (64)	11 (59)

Source: Sense and Sensibilities: Public Opinion and the BBFC Guidelines, bBBFC

Sexual violence

The BBFC has a strict policy on rape and sexual violence. Where the portrayal eroticises or endorses sexual assault, the Board is likely to require cuts at any classification level. This is more likely with video than film, because video scenes can be replayed repeatedly. Any association of sex with non-consensual restraint, pain or humiliation may be cut.

Imitable techniques

The BBFC is also concerned about detailed portrayal of criminal and violent techniques and the glamorisation of weapons. The use of weapons which are easily accessible to young people will be restricted. Imitable combat techniques may be cut. Any action which would be likely to promote illegal or anti-social behaviour in real life is of particular concern. Imitable detail of criminal techniques may be unacceptable at any classification level. Potentially dangerous activity presented as safe and exciting is of particular concern in works aimed at children. The BBFC is most concerned about videos, where a technique can be watched again and again until the lesson is learned.

Horror

Horror films are subject to the same Guideline constraints as all other films. The BBFC recognises that audiences pay to see horror films because they like being frightened. The Board does not cut films simply because they alarm or shock. Instead, it classifies them to ensure that the young and vulnerable are protected.

Drugs

No work taken as a whole, even at '18', may promote or encourage the use of illegal drugs. Clear instructive detail is unacceptable at all levels up to '15'. Even at '18', such detail may only be acceptable if there are exceptional considerations of context. Glamorising detail is a particular concern. The dangers of showing instructive detail are particularly acute in videos where scenes can be replayed over and over again.

• The above information is from the BBFC's web site which can be found at www.bbfc.org.uk Alternatively, see page 41 for their address details.

© British Board of Film Classification (BBFC)

Film sex rules to be eased

By Nigel Reynolds, Arts Correspondent

Film censors will unveil plans today to relax rules on sex and violence in adult films and videos but to take a tougher line on entertainment for children and teenagers.

The British Board of Film Classification is also expected to crack down on scenes in films that show drug-taking. New research by the board has shown that both adults and teenagers are increasingly concerned about episodes concerning drugs. Even though drug-taking is now widespread in society, the board will tell film-makers that scenes which contain any element of 'instruction' about drugs and how to acquire them or use them risk being cut.

The BBFC has faced calls by MPs and others for it to be wound up and for the Government to take over responsibility for film classification. The 'liberal Left' has continued to argue for film-makers to be left free of censorship but there has been growing unease among middle-of-the-road cinema-goers about the effect of film violence and sex.

Defendants in several court cases have claimed that they committed violent crimes under the influence of a film or a film character. Soon after Jack Straw became Home Secretary, he clashed with the board, notably its outgoing director James Ferman, over moves to relax censorship on pornographic videos. There was also public anger that the BBFC sanctioned films such as David Cronenberg's *Crash*, based on a J. G. Ballard novel, and the French film *Romance*.

The former showed people getting sexual thrills out of causing car crashes. *Romance*, made in France and said to be the most sexually explicit mainstream film ever shot, was released only after heavy cuts in France but was passed uncut in Britain. The new rules announced today are an attempt to quell criticism.

The BBFC will publish tougher guidelines for film-makers on what is permissible and what is not for films seen by the young – the films eligible for U, PG, 12 and 15 ratings. The guidelines are based on commissioned research into public attitudes.

The board is understood to have reached the view that there should be relatively little interference over what adults should be allowed to watch at the cinema. The board believes this will not open the floodgates to extreme violence and pornography in cinemas because mainstream film studios, multiplex chains and distributors will see little commercial advantage in shocking middle-of-the-road audiences.

© Telegraph Group Limited, London 2000

Sense and sensibilities

Public opinion and the BBFC Guidelines

British Board of Film Classification

Bad language

- 56% of the national sample agreed that 'young people use bad language because of what they hear in films and videos'.
- 48% of the national sample thought that the language Guidelines were 'about right' (43% thought they were not strict enough, and only 5% thought they were too strict).
- Both sets of juries were concerned about bad language, especially in the junior categories. There was some concern about the use of 'very strong language' at '15'.

Sex

- 46% of the national sample agreed that 'people over 18 have a right to see graphic portrayals of real sex in films and videos'.
- 54% of the national sample thought that the Guidelines for sex were 'about right' (32% thought they were not strict enough, and 12% thought they were too strict). The consensus of both juries was that some relaxation in sex Guidelines was possible, especially at '15' and '18'.

Violence

- 46% of the national sample agreed with the statement that 'watching violence in films generally makes people more likely to be violent in real life'. When members of the citizens' juries were asked their views on that statement at the outset of the jury process, half of them agreed with it. However, nearly three-quarters of them disagreed with it once they had heard the evidence of the 'expert witnesses'.
- 46% of the national sample agreed that 'violence is more acceptable if it occurs in comic, historic or fantastic settings'.
- 51% of the national sample thought that the violence Guidelines were 'about right' (42% thought they were not strict enough, and only 5% thought they were too strict).

Drugs

- 52% of the national sample agreed that 'films should be allowed to portray drug use in a realistic manner'. The portrayal of drug use was considered more offensive than all other classification issues (sex, violence, language, nudity and blasphemy).
- 47% of the national sample thought that the drugs Guidelines were not strict enough (45% thought that they were 'about right', and only 4% thought they were too strict). Members of the citizens' juries also felt that the Guidelines were too relaxed, particularly at '12', and that more differentiation between hard and soft drugs was needed. Concern also extended to the '15' and '18' categories, with 46% of the national sample agreeing that the Guidelines were not strict enough even at '18'.

Methodology

Several techniques were used to maximise the range of people consulted during the research programme, and to achieve a combination of quantitative and qualitative input:

- Citizens' juries
- National survey
- Roadshow/postal questionnaires
- Web site questionnaires

• The above information is an extract from *Sense and Sensibilities – Public Opinion & the BBFC Guidelines*, a report produced by the BBFC on research into public attitudes to taste and decency within the classification process and the BBFC's new revised Guidelines. The report is available on their web site at www.bbfc.co.uk or see page 41 for their address details.

© British Board of Film Classification (BBFC)

The classifications

Information from the British Board of Film Classification (BBFC)

'U' – UNIVERSAL

Suitable for all

It is impossible to predict what might upset any particular child. But a 'U' film should be suitable for audiences aged four years and over. Works aimed at children should be set within a positive moral framework and should offer reassuring counter-balances to any violence, threat or horror.

Theme – Treatment of problematic themes must be sensitive and appropriate to a younger audience.

Language – Infrequent use only of very mild bad language.

Nudity – Occasional natural nudity, with no sexual context.

Sex – Mild sexual behaviour (e.g. kissing) and references only (e.g. to 'making love').

Violence – Mild violence only. Occasional mild threat or menace only.

Imitable Techniques – No emphasis on realistic weapons.

Horror – Horror effects should be mild and brief and should take account of the presence of very young viewers. The outcome should be reassuring.

Drugs – No references to illegal drugs or drug use.

'Uc'

Videos classified 'uc' are particularly suitable for pre-school children.

'PG'

General viewing, but some scenes may be unsuitable for some children. Unaccompanied children of any age may watch. A 'PG' film should not disturb a child aged around eight or older. However, parents are advised to consider whether the content may upset younger or more sensitive children.

Theme – More serious issues may be featured, e.g. crime, domestic violence, racism (providing nothing in their treatment condones them).

Language – Mild bad language only.

Nudity – Natural nudity, with no sexual context.

Sex – Sexual activity may be implied, but should be discreet and infrequent. Mild sexual references and innuendo only.

Violence – Moderate violence, without detail, may be allowed – if justified by its setting (e.g. historic, comedy or fantasy).

Imitable Techniques – No glamorisation of realistic, contemporary weapons. No detail of fighting or other dangerous techniques.

Horror – Frightening sequences should not be prolonged or intense. Fantasy settings may be a mitigating factor.

Drugs – No references to illegal drugs or drug use unless entirely innocuous.

'12'

Suitable only for 12 years and over

No one younger than 12 may see a '12' film in a cinema or rent or buy a '12' rated video.

Theme – Mature themes are acceptable, but their treatment must be suitable for young teenagers.

Language – The use of strong language (e.g. 'fuck') should be rare and must be justified by context.

Nudity – Nudity is allowed, but in a sexual context will be brief and discreet.

Sex – Sexual activity may be implied. Sexual references may reflect the familiarity of most adolescents today with sex education through school.

Violence – Violence must not dwell on detail. There should be no emphasis on injuries or blood. Sexual violence may only be implied or briefly indicated and without physical detail.

Imitable Techniques – Dangerous techniques (examples include: combat, hanging, suicides) should contain no imitable detail. Realistic and contemporary weapons should not be glamorised.

Horror – Sustained threat and menace is permitted. Occasional gory moments only.

Drugs – Brief and occasional references to, and sight of, 'soft' drug-taking (e.g. cannabis) are allowed, but must be justified by context and should indicate the dangers. No instructional elements are permitted.

'15'

Suitable only for 15 years and over

No one younger than 15 may see a '15' film in a cinema or rent or buy a '15' rated video.

Theme – No theme is prohibited, provided the treatment is appropriate to 15-year-olds.

Language – There may be frequent use of strong language; the strongest terms (e.g. 'cunt') are only rarely acceptable. Continued aggressive use of strong language and sexual abuse is unacceptable.

Nudity – There are no constraints on nudity in a non-sexual or educational context.

Sex – Sexual activity and nudity may be portrayed but without strong detail. The depiction of casual sex should be handled responsibly. There may be occasional strong verbal references to sexual behaviour.

Violence – Violence may be strong but may not dwell on the infliction of pain, and of injuries. Scenes of sexual violence must be discreet and brief.

Imitable Techniques – Dangerous combat techniques such as ear claps, head-butts and blows to the neck are unlikely to be acceptable. There may be no emphasis on the use of easily accessible lethal weapons (in particular, knives).

Horror – Sustained or detailed infliction of pain or injury is unacceptable.

Drugs – Drug taking may be shown but clear instructive detail is unacceptable. The film as a whole must not promote or encourage drug use.

'18'
Suitable only for adults

No one younger than 18 may see an '18' film in a cinema or rent or buy an '18' rated video.

The BBFC respects the right of adults to chose their own entertainment, within the law. It will therefore expect to intervene only rarely in relation to '18' rated cinema films. In the case of videos, which are more accessible to younger viewers, intervention may be more frequent. There are no constraints at this level on theme, language, nudity or horror. The Board may, however, cut or reject the following content

- any detailed portrayal of violent or dangerous acts which is likely to promote the activity. This includes also instructive detail of illegal drug use
- the more explicit images of sexual activity – unless they can be exceptionally justified by context

Sex Education at '18'
Where sex material genuinely seeks to inform and educate in matters such as human sexuality, safe sex and health, exceptions to the normal constraints on explicit images may be made in the public interest. Such explicit detail must be kept to the minimum necessary to illustrate the educational or instructional points being made.

Sex Works at '18'
Material which appears to be simulated is generally passed '18', while images of real sex are confined to the 'R18' category.

'R18'
The following content is not acceptable
- Any material which is in breach of the criminal law
- Material likely to encourage an interest in abusive sexual activity (e.g. paedophilia, incest) which may include depictions involving adults role-playing as non-adults
- The portrayal of any sexual activity, whether real or simulated, which involves lack of consent
- The infliction of pain or physical harm, real or (in a sexual context) simulated. Some allowance may be made for mild consensual activity
- Any sexual threats or humiliation which do not form part of a clearly consenting role-playing game
- The use of any form of physical restraint which prevents participants from withdrawing consent, for example, ball gags
- Penetration by any object likely to cause actual harm or associated with violence
- Activity which is degrading or dehumanising (examples include the portrayal of bestiality, necrophilia, defecation, urolagnia)

The following content, subject to the above, may be permitted
- Aroused genitalia
- Masturbation
- Oral-genital contact including kissing, licking and sucking
- Penetration by finger, penis, tongue, vibrator or dildo
- Non-harmful fetish material
- Group sexual activity
- Ejaculation and semen

These guidelines make no distinction between heterosexual and homosexual activity.

• The above information is an extract from the BBFC's web site which can be found at www.bbfc.org.uk

Child guinea pigs to view 'adult' film scenes

Film censorship: youngsters to be asked for their reactions to 'explicit' material to see if current movie classifications work

Thousands of schoolchildren are to be shown film clips featuring violence, drug abuse and sexually explicit language in an experimental programme that could pave the way for a further relaxation of the UK's censorship rules.

The British Board of Film Classification is already under attack for relaxing its guidelines to allow more casual sex, horror and violence to be shown in 15-certificate movies.

Now it is inviting children from around the UK to special screenings designed to judge the success of its decisions, and to help it to decide whether to go even further.

By gauging their reaction to scenes involving such 'adult' behaviour as sex and drug-taking from films already available to them, it hopes to make up its mind whether to make the current 12 category advisory, as with the PG rating.

Around 250 children aged 15 to 18 will attend the first screening, which is to be held next month in east London.

The excerpts to be shown include scenes from movies that narrowly missed out on 18 certificates because of their disturbing content. In one sequence, taken from horror movie *Valentine*, a scantily clad young woman is murdered by a maniac wielding a power drill, while another, from the gothic fantasy *Sleepy Hollow*, depicts a small boy hiding beneath the floorboards of a house while his family is slain by a headless horseman.

The screening will also include strong scenes cut from from TV broadcasts such as teen horror *Buffy the Vampire Slayer* and *The Simpsons*. While these scenes are not shown on British TV they are available on videos of the show. Each clip will be preceded by a brief warning and an explanation of the context in which it appears in the film from which it is taken.

AH - WE WERE RIGHT, THAT FILM CLIP WASN'T SUITABLE FOR THAT AGE-GROUP...

Ros Bates, the senior BBFC examiner behind the new initiative, said it was introduced to give children direct say in film regulation which, until now, has been reserved for adults.

'Before we issued our revised guidelines last year, we held our first proper public consultation, but we talked only to adults at that stage,' she said. 'The guidelines aren't set in stone, and from now on we are planning periodic reviews. With this in mind it was suggested that we should really be asking for the views of the biggest audience for films and videos: adolescents. We want to find out what 15- to 18-year-olds think about our classification decisions and whether they believe we're getting them right. After they have seen the clips we will be asking them to fill in questionnaires.

'We obviously won't be showing the children anything from an 18 film, but we have deliberately chosen clips that address more adult themes, some of them from films that were borderline when it came to deciding which certificate they should be given. Taking material out of context is always problematic, but we will do our best to warn the children of anything scary or risqué and to set the context for them.'

Miss Bates said that, as well as expressing their own views on the excerpts, it was hoped that the children would be able to comment on how their younger siblings might be affected. Over the coming months a further nine screenings, or 'junior roadshows', would be held nationwide, some of them aimed at younger children.

News of the screenings has drawn a mixed response from parents and child protection groups. Arthur Cornell, chairman of the Family Education Trust, a charity which promotes traditional family values, said: 'I think it's quite difficult to sit children down and ask them to assess what is and what isn't good for them. No youngster watching one of these clips is going to say, "oh, that frightened me dreadfully", because it's not cool to say that.'

Eileen Hayes, parenting adviser for the NSPCC, which opposes the prospective changes to the 12 classification, added: 'Parents increasingly have less influence over their children's lives, especially when it comes to screen violence. Although research on the links between film violence and behaviour is inconclusive, parents feel the need to be cautious.

'The BBFC excuses the relaxation of certificates by saying that children are growing up faster, but the reality is that we are forcing them to do so by exposing them to more adult images. Parents who want control over their children's viewing will find this proposal undermining.'

'We need to know about these things, they are part of life'

By James Morrison

'I don't understand what all the fuss was about with *Nightmare on Elm Street* or *The Exorcist*, and I just found *Pulp Fiction* funny,' said 17-year-old movie fan Inam Mahmood. 'But that scene in *Sleepy Hollow* was pushing it for a 15. I'd have made it an 18 on the basis of that bit.'

Inam is one of a group of teenagers from east London whose frequently incisive, if occasionally contradictory, views will help the British Board of Film Classification to plot the future course of film censorship.

Next month, students on the BTEC National Diploma media course at Newham Sixth Form College, Plaistow, will form part of the first of 10 pioneering children's viewing panels being organised by the BBFC.

In order to give them a sneak preview of the event, *The Independent on Sunday* arranged to show them some of the excerpts they will be asked to judge.

While many of the chosen scenes prompted mild amusement from the students, some provoked far stronger reactions. Several people were particularly critical of the scene from *Sleepy Hollow* in which a small boy cowers in horror as a headless horseman massacres his entire family, before turning his axe towards him.

Maria Lam, 17, said: 'Looking at that sequence I think its rating should be raised to an 18, because the whole family was killed, and even if the young boy had stayed alive he would have been severely traumatised by this ordeal.'

Sheeza Latif, 18, dissented, saying the sequence should be viewed in the context of a film that was meant to be a far-fetched fantasy: 'If you try too hard to limit what children see in films, you are going to have kids who go to all sorts of lengths to see these things anyway, so you have to be realistic.'

A brief scene from 12-rated action adventure *The Mummy* in which a man's tongue is pulled out by red hot tongs also drew a mixed reaction. While some students said that they thought the idea was too disturbing for a film aimed at children younger than 12, others praised the careful editing that left most of the incident to the viewer's imagination.

A scene from coming-of-age comedy *American Pie* in which a suburban father gives his son a pep talk on the birds and the bees drew

---

The full list of excerpts to be shown at the first screening on 10 July is as follows:

Romeo Must Die (15) – fight sequence

Buffy the Vampire Slayer (15) – uncut video scene censored for early evening TV

The Simpsons (PG) – uncut video sequence

Josh (12) – fight sequence in Hindi film

American Pie (15) – scene in which dad talks to son about sex

Picture Perfect (PG) – spoken references to sexual activity

The Mummy (12) – punishment scene in which the victim's tongue is cut out

Vertical Limit (12) – father offering to sacrifice himself for his two teenage sons as all three hang from cliff edge

Valentine (15) – a girl in a swimming suit being killed by power drill-wielding murderer

Sleepy Hollow (15) – a young boy hides under floorboards as headless horseman kills his family

Forces of Nature (12) – teenagers smoking cannabis

Dude Where's My Car? (15) – a dog smoking cannabis

---

laughter for its mixture of lewd references and more subtle innuendo. Sapna Degan, 18, said that, if anything, the film's rating should be dropped from a 15 to a 12 because of its 'educational value'. She said: 'It's about growing up and it's aimed at young people.'

Scenes of sustained but non-bloody violence in 15-rated martial arts movie *Romeo Must Die* drew a similarly measured response.

However, there were conflicting views on the question of censorship in general, and moves to relax the criteria for 12 films in particular. While there was a consensus that violence and psychological horror should be limited in movies aimed at younger age groups, a more relaxed attitude was taken to sex, nudity and drug use.

Maria said she believed that movie censors still had an important role to play, but added: 'If you don't ever show drugs in films under 15, kids are going to grow up without knowing about them, and one day they'll ask, "mummy, what are drugs?"'

Sheeza added: 'Violence isn't natural, but sex is. Children need to grow up knowing about things like that, and they need to know about drugs too. I saw the film *Kids* and it had lots of drugs and sex in it, but this is part of life for a lot of young people.'

A note of caution was sounded by 18-year-old Scott Clements, who said: 'Just because we've grown up where we have in London, and we may be desensitised to some things that happen around us, other kids may come from more old-fashioned backgrounds, so they may not be able to take so much.'

Uzma Hussain, 18, added: 'I remember seeing *Nightmare on Elm Street* when I was 13 or 14. I complained to my parents so much that they said, "all right, you can watch it then", and afterwards I wished I hadn't, because it was so scary.'

Television and sex

Information from mediawatch-uk

Introduction

The past few years have seen an increase in the number of charges brought by women against men for sexual harassment, a rise in the number of rapes and a coarsening in attitudes generally between men and women, of which a lack of basic courtesy and respect is only one aspect. We have also seen a growing contempt for the principle of lasting marriage based on mutual commitment, and a widespread feeling that men and women are entitled to be sexually irresponsible and selfish if they so desire, with no thought for the people who might be affected by their actions. These include discarded sexual partners, spouses and the most vulnerable group, children.

If we are to be tough on these issues in our attempt to create a better society, we must be equally tough on their causes. Many observers – expert commentators and ordinary people alike – see TV as a major influence. They point to a clear link between our attitudes to other people as sex objects and the way some very particular attitudes to sex – which would simply not have been tolerated a few decades ago – are now being actively promoted as perfectly normal in the soaps, dramas, movies and comedy programmes we see every day on TV. In addition to this there is the proliferation of satellite and cable channels, originating from this country and elsewhere, licensed and unlicensed by UK authorities, which continue to transmit pornographic material seemingly subject to only tenuous regulation.

Many people in the broadcasting industry, and a number of leading politicians, still refuse to recognise any connection between what we see on TV and our behaviour. No wonder. For them to admit a clear cause and effect would mean they would have to admit that they have been wrong about a major cause of social ill and then strengthen the regulations.

As an organisation we are against the idea of Government censorship. We believe in effective self-regulation which is upheld and respected. What we want is a sympathetic climate of sensitivity and respect for others, in which forethought and self-restraint are practised by the broadcasters and everyone involved in the creative process, including directors, writers and actors. We believe that most of the viewing public would welcome a general raising of moral tone.

> *If we are to be tough on these issues in our attempt to create a better society, we must be equally tough on their causes*

Most of us already accept a number of constraints on our behaviour as part of living in civilised society – how we drive our cars, where we put our litter, how much noise we make and so on. Of course these constraints do effectively 'censor' our behaviour but we can understand, and go along with, the principle of advancing the common good that lay behind them. The idea of self-restraint is at the heart of a caring society. It is far preferable that any decision to restrain behaviour comes from the individual, rather than official bureaucracy. It preserves self-respect.

We now need to accept this kind of restraint in our entertainment too, if we are to build a caring society in which marriage is given its proper value once more and people accept full responsibility for the consequences of their sexual behaviour. If we don't even try, we certainly won't see it happen.

Sex on TV

Storytelling, and listening to stories, is an intrinsic part of our human nature. Morality tales, with good triumphing over evil, are one tradition which is alive and well. The love story is another. The classic romance, in which the hero and the heroine meet, fall in love and then have to decide whether to get married or not, and resolve their other relationships, is as old as time.

We all identify with love stories and enjoy them at different levels of sophistication depending on our taste and maturity. In the absence of any moral guidance, we also draw on them as a resource to help us work

Public awareness and views on regulation

Although two-thirds of under 55-year-olds felt that viewers should be most responsible for regulation, agreement decreased with age: only 55% of over 65-year-olds felt the same. Broadcasters or programme-makers were thought to be responsible for controlling television content by twice as many people as expected government or regulators to take responsibility.

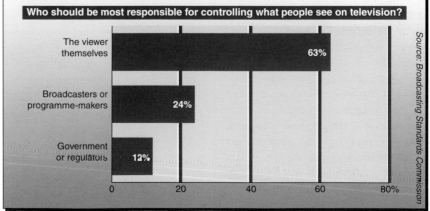

Who should be most responsible for controlling what people see on television?

- The viewer themselves: 63%
- Broadcasters or programme-makers: 24%
- Government or regulators: 12%

Source: Broadcasting Standards Commission

out how we should conduct our own lives. In short, we need them.

The issue, then, is not with the love story itself, but how it is told on TV and film and video. We recognise that there is a clear difference between the images each of us finds erotic, and images which are pornographic. What we find erotic is highly personal and can be quite neutral in its own right, like the face of our loved one or our favourite TV celebrity. Or it can be an image which is intended to titillate us, like the footage of semi-naked bodies shown at tea time on *Bay Watch*! Either way, we do not say such things are pornographic in themselves!

But graphic sex on TV is pornographic. It undermines respect for human dignity – hence it is pornographic in the literal sense – because we become desensitised by it. Many people – of all faiths and none – say they find the all-out portrayal of sex on TV offensive, because its deliberate portrayal assumes the audience is without imagination.

What about nudity on TV? This is an important issue too. As a guideline, the state of undress that we accept in the street is what is appropriate on our screens. TV is a public arena, not a private one.

Two key events in the 1960s had a major impact on the way we discuss these things. The first key event was the ineptly handled obscenity trial of *Lady Chatterley's Lover*, D. H. Lawrence's least impressive book. This ended in failure for the Crown and the ridiculing of the new Obscene Publications Act. The second key event was the end of official censorship in the theatre at around the same time. The new 'permissive' atmosphere of the 1960s meant that writers, producers and directors could reveal more of the characters' sexual activities, liaisons and misadventures, without risk of prosecution owing to badly worded law.

The lack of moral leadership gave people the chance to think about changing attitudes to sex before marriage. But in the 1960s, portrayal of the sex act itself remained largely confined to 'porn' films, the preserve of seedy men in dirty raincoats and cheeky schoolboys furtively venturing down the back streets of Soho and elsewhere.

In Britain there was still very much a 'seaside postcard' attitude to sex at the cinema. Feature films tended to be suggestive rather than graphically revealing. The audience knew what the characters were up to but we didn't expect to see them doing it. Even in *The Graduate*, what Ben (Dustin Hoffman) did to Mrs Robinson (Anne Bancroft) was mostly left to our imaginations. The sex scene as we know it first reached its current prominence in the 1970s, with a wave of Hollywood directors who started pushing it to new heights of explicitness. And here, in Britain, our directors caught on too knowing that they could also get away with it.

Compare the relative innocence of films like *The Knack (And How To Get It)* or *Georgie Girl*, with the sophistication of *A Touch of Class*, a few short years later, in which George Segal is married with children but is intent on playing around with Glenda Jackson, who is divorced with children. And yet, before they become entangled she asks him if he knows what he is doing. Her attitude suggests that though divorced, she still has a basic concern about breaking up his marriage. In any case, this sort of thing passed largely unnoticed in Britain at the time. In the 1970s the British Board of Film Censors was justifiably more concerned with the likes of *A Clockwork Orange* and *The Devils*.

Meanwhile playwrights and TV writers flourished in the freer atmosphere of the 1970s. Some would say that Dennis Potter, in particular, made his reputation for pushing back the barriers, following on from the tradition of the 'Plays For Today' of the 1960s – dramas which led to Mary Whitehouse founding the National Viewers' And Listeners' Association.

The impact these TV dramas enjoyed was soon to be eclipsed by the impact of video technology. In the 1980s, with the arrival of the video recorder in four out of five homes, it was suddenly possible to capture all the more explicit films on tape and see them at one's leisure – rewinding and replaying the exciting bits to our heart's content. With the video recorder, suddenly there simply wasn't enough on TV to keep people amused. So during the 1980s video rental shops and video 'sell-through' arrived on our high streets in a big way. The cinema box office suffered for a while as consumers discovered the convenience of catching up on the recent films at home. (It has caught up since, as people realise the limitations of the small screen.) Digital technology will enable much larger domestic TV screens and sophisticated audio equipment is now available to give cinema-quality stereo sound. With the video retailer effectively acting as the moral guardian, there was a clear difference between what was acceptable on TV and what could have a video release. With such a choice now available – and with so little regulation – ultimately the viewer became even more blasé about sex on TV. And the morality behind it was accepted too!

The films themselves were much 'darker' in tone. The Glenn Close character in *Fatal Attraction*, made in the late 1980s, couldn't care two hoots about breaking up Michael Douglas' marriage after a fling. She was a far cry from the Glenda Jackson character in *A Touch Of Class*, who did care, as we have mentioned.

TV broadcasting also expanded in the 1980s, with the launch of Channel 4, which was given a 'bad boy' manifesto from Day 1. Interestingly the first ads C4 showed were for a brand of videotape! The Government was under pressure to act from National VALA and others, and the result was the formation of the Broadcasting Standards Council. But generally speaking this has taken a lenient view of a worsening situation, which some say has been caused by the broadcasting

authorities' failure to regulate effectively and contriving Codes of Practice that permit maximum latitude in terms of taste and decency in programmes.

In the 1990s, movies on TV became ever more important in attracting an audience to please the advertisers. Led by Channel 4 the TV companies also became directly involved with film production, so that they could be guaranteed first showing. Some of these films reflected clearly the attitudes of the broadcasters behind them. Channel 4's biggest film production success so far has been *Four Weddings And A Funeral*, a comedy in which the leading character – played by Hugh Grant – is pathologically unable to commit himself to marriage. This attitude, the film tells us in a script full of F-words, is now acceptable! But *Four Weddings And Funeral* wasn't the worst of it, by any means. In 1996, James Ferman, the then Director of the British Board of Film Classification, said publicly that he felt helpless to control the nature of the films coming our way from Hollywood – all of which were bound to end up on our TV screens sooner or later after their cinema release. Sadly, this remark, and his further remark that we must hope that Hollywood wakes up with a conscience, brought no suggestion that the Government might intervene.

Film censor or no film censor, the important point is that the current TV regulations are ineffective in dealing with sex on TV. The BBC's Royal Charter, governing BBC1, BBC2, and any other 'narrowcast' channels the BBC may operate in the near future, is largely powerless to temper the more bold creative brains and commissioners of programmes. And the independent contractors can see equally clearly that the Broadcasting Act can do nothing directly to curtail their excesses.

In the late 1990s the wheel is turning still further, with the arrival of Channel 5, numerous satellite and cable TV channels and the digital expansion that is in prospect. How on earth can all these channels be controlled and breaches of good taste and decency redressed? No one can

possibly watch them all and see all the programmes. We are faced with a new situation which has arisen without any real public or parliamentary debate: the onus for maintaining standards is shifting away from the broadcasting authorities to ordinary viewers and listeners who will be expected to write and complain every time offence has been caused. Since no objective standards of good taste and decency seem to apply the only measure of dissatisfaction will be the number of protests from the public received by the broadcasting authorities. And the outcome of such protestation, as is well known, is at best uncertain and most often rejected.

It is true that the police still crack down on the really obscene videos. But when it comes to the ever bolder 'run-of-the-mill' sex scenes shown on TV, the bemused audience is presented with two choices – like it and keep watching, or lump it and turn off. We say that's ridiculous. We believe that an overhaul of the Obscene Publications Act is long overdue – the only legal measure left to enable action against sex on TV – to strengthen and update the law effectively.

• The above information is an excerpt from *Television and Sex*, a booklet produced by mediawatch-uk. See page 41 for their address details.

© *mediawatch-uk*

TV film viewers want information not censorship

By Jason Deans

A new survey on attitudes to censorship of films screened on TV suggests that viewers want less intervention and more information. The survey, *Making Sense of Censorship* commissioned by FilmFour, found that while viewers have concerns over violence within feature films on TV, they are able to distinguish between real and cartoon, or escapist, violence.

Respondents said they wanted less intervention from legislators, but more facts and information from broadcasters so they could make their own informed decisions about which films to watch.

The survey also revealed there is more concern about growing access to the internet and control of video stores than the content of films on TV.

The study also found that:

• 64% believed the internet was a more significant issue than TV
• 77% stated that cutting TV movies is the least favoured method of regulating the content, with warnings and information prior to transmission the preferred approach
• 82% believed it was their responsibility to decide what was acceptable viewing for their families and households, a figure that rose to 98% in homes with children
• 64% believed existing censorship legislation was unclear, while insufficient information was available to allow self-regulation

• *Making Sense of Censorship* was based on more than 900 interviews carried out by TWResearch. The survey will be presented in full at a conference taking place today at the ICA in London.

© *Guardian Newspapers Limited 2000*

More sex, please, we're British filmgoers

**By Fiachra Gibbons,
Arts Correspondent**

The censor is to take a much more relaxed attitude to sex in 18 certificate films in the first formal loosening of Britain's relatively prudish screen code.

The British Board of Film Classification said yesterday it would now 'only rarely' cut explicit scenes after a six-month consultation process found the public would rather make up their own minds about what was acceptable.

But the new liberal mood to sex – which extends to some degree to violence – disguises a far more restrictive line on drugs and bad language in films aimed at younger audiences.

In the commercially crucial 15 category – where the board has frequently been at loggerheads with film-makers who view the 18 certificate as a box office death sentence – strong language will 'only be rarely acceptable'.

After the recent furore over the 'ludicrous' 18 rating given to *The End of the Affair*, there is to be a more permissive attitude to sex in 15 certificate films.

Significantly, however, the relaxation applies only to its depiction in 'responsible, loving and developing relationships'. Casual sex, the board warns, should be 'handled responsibly'.

Last night Pact, the producers' alliance which represents the bulk of British film-makers, gave the changes a cautious welcome but claimed there was a 'touch of moral panic about them'.

> **But the new liberal mood to sex – which extends to some degree to violence – disguises a far more restrictive line on drugs and bad language in films aimed at younger audiences**

The guidelines show their teeth in the depiction of drug use. All mention of them in U films and videos will be banned, references severely curtailed at PG, 12 and 15 levels, while scenes akin to those in *Trainspotting* which give 'instructive detail' in 18 certificate films will be cut.

Robin Duval, the BBFC's director, revealed that if Quentin Tarantino's *Pulp Fiction* – in which John Travolta played a hitman with a heroin habit – came before him now, he would consider cutting it.

Mr Duval admitted that with film-makers like Tarantino and his many imitators there were 'difficult calls to be made between promoting and portraying violence'. He said the board was now prepared to 'take extreme action' against films which promoted such cruelty.

The board's president, Andreas Whittam Smith, who is seen as steering a more conservative course than the previous regime under James Ferman, said he had worries about the blurring of the line between 'comic or stylised violence' and scenes which revelled and gloried in it.

He said he aimed to alter the guidelines every few years in line with changing attitudes, but warned that this 'does not mean they will shift in the same direction'.

The new rules were 'not a sea change' but simply a clarification of the way decisions were now made. Even so, Mr Whittam Smith ad-

mitted the BBFC would still find itself 'in a pickle' with the growing trend towards 'naturalistic' sex scenes in arthouse films like *Romance* and *Seul Contre Tous*. He said the board would never be able to pass anything which conflicted with the Obscene Publications Act.

But he made a stout defence of the board's decision to be less proscriptive about sex scenes in 15 films.

'We have the toughest guidelines in the world on film already and still we have the highest level of teenage pregnancy,' he said. 'We have the power to intervene and cut which they do not have abroad, we have mandatory certification, and we also control the video market.'

The BBFC's decision to err on the side of tolerance at 18 comes after it was forced to relax the rules on sex videos after being defeated in the high court earlier this year. The explicit R18 films are available only through licensed sex shops.

Censorship . . . and sensibility

Sex
The End Of The Affair – and Ralph Fiennes' offending buttocks – will now pass as 15 rather than getting an 18 rating, while the difficulty in passing 'real sex' scenes in arthouse films like *The Idiots* and *Romance* are now eased because they can be 'exceptionally justified by context'.

Violence
The more liberal line on the 18 rating means *The Fight Club*, in which Brad Pitt and Edward Norton starred as corporate suits who relaxed through bare-knuckle boxing, would now pass uncut. *Last House on the Left*, the only film the BBFC refused to certify this year, would still not pass because of its 'incendiary mix of sex and violence'.

Drugs
Several scenes in *Trainspotting* which could be interpreted as giving 'instructional detail' on drug-taking could now go, while 'if *Pulp Fiction* were to come to us now, we would look at that scene where we see John Travolta in a car high on heroin with a little more concern'.

But the new guidelines themselves follow a study, *Sense and Sensibilities*, commissioned by the board a year ago into public attitudes.

The research showed 56% of those surveyed thought young people used bad language because of what they heard in films. Nearly half, however, thought adults should be allowed to watch real sex on the screen.

Do you really want more censorship?

Information from Feminists Against Censorship

Women need open and safe communication about sexual matters including the power relations of sex. We don't need new forms of guilt parading under the banner of political correctness. We need a safe legal working environment for sex workers, not repressive laws or an atmosphere of social stigma that empowers police and punters to brutalise them. We need sexually explicit material produced by and for women, freed from the control of moral conservatives and misogynists, whether they sit on the board of directors or the board of censors. We need an analysis of violence that empowers women and protects them at the same time. We need a feminism willing to tackle issues of class and race and to deal with the variety of oppressions in the world, not to reduce all oppression to pornography.

What is censorship?
Censorship is something that is imposed from above by those who seek to control us by limiting what we can know. In essence, it is an attempt to constrain what we think and believe. By silencing the voices of dissent, those in power hope to suppress criticism of their policies and programmes.

What is wrong with censorship?
Knowledge is power, and censorship takes that power away from ordinary people and concentrates it in the hands of the censors. Censorship harms us all.

Where is it?
In more places than you probably think. For example, you may not know how often images and other content are removed from television shows, videos, and 18-rated films.

You might not even be aware that information and issues that reach your daily newspaper are limited to fit into the commercial and political interests of the owners and their friends in business and government.

What kinds of things are censored?
Typical examples are things that express criticism or opposition to the state, to major commercial interests, and to religious or moral 'authorities'.

This covers opposition across a broad political spectrum. Educational material is frequently suppressed.

So, why 'feminists against censorship'?
Feminists have long recognised that censorship hurts women, restricting debate that challenges the status quo

and particularly affecting material created by women to educate and inform about sexual matters. Sexual censorship in particular has always been popular with governments when suppressing activists who wish to confront racism and sexism.

During the 1980s, the moral right exploited women's fears about sexual violence and promoted the view that pornography was the cause of the problem and therefore censorship the solution. The government seized upon this as a means to appear to care about women's safety without spending any money. Some pro-censorship women also adopted this view, saying that all women wish to see greater censorship, and claiming that this was the only feminist position. This seemed to have virtually shut down any debate about censorship. The women who formed FAC in 1989 were feminists whose roots were firmly based in the 1960s civil rights movement. Their impetus came from concern that feminism was moving further away from women's sexual liberation towards a more narrow and traditional view of women as victims. FAC was instrumental in reviving concerns about censorship itself and reminding people that sex was not our enemy. We believe that an environment where many ideas and viewpoints flourish encourages social progress, and that censorship inhibits social change. History has taught us that censorship is most often used by the powerful against those who are oppressed and struggling to be heard. Censorship is what helps preserve the status quo. As feminists we should be speaking out against censorship, whatever form it takes.

But the danger still exists

However, despite our success, the state has continued to churn out new examples of censorship – satellite television channels and computer-generated images, non-certificated films and videos – and new police powers to invade people's homes in search of erotic materials. The government also wants to censor the Internet. And journalists have been imprisoned for 'conspiracy to incite criminal damage' by reporting animal liberation actions.

But isn't pornography harmful?

Despite various claims, no one has ever been able to demonstrate that pornography causes harm. But isn't it strange that we assume sexual imagery is dangerous? After all, it's essentially material that's designed to arouse people sexually, and that isn't a bad thing in itself. There is no evidence that it causes violence or makes people behave anti-socially. Even the 1990 Home Office report did not find any link between porn and rape or violence.

Of course, some people dislike porn, but that is no reason to say others can't have it. FAC believes that using porn should be an individual choice.

But isn't pornography just for guys?

No. Pornography is material that is intended to sexually arouse. That's what's sold under the name of 'pornography', and that's what people expect to see when they look for 'pornography'.

But in the United Kingdom, the obscenity laws make it so tricky to produce highly charged erotic material that producers and distributors only feel safe showing images of women on their own – for fear of prosecution – rather than showing mutual activity between partners. Obviously, these are most likely to appeal to the tastes of heterosexual men. The largest distributor in Britain long refused to carry any picture of an aroused man or any picture showing two or more people together. So the 'for men only' appearance of pornography is really a result of censoriousness, not something fundamental to the genre.

In recent years, women have been producing their own erotic material, and FAC welcomes this. But producing anything outside the norm is still a gamble, as you never know what's going to be prosecuted. Erotic material that challenges the mainstream traditions is the kind that's most likely to be attacked by reactionaries and by the police in particular.

Don't children need protecting?

Yes – from ignorance. Research on sex offenders shows that sexual ignorance and repression is an important factor in their back-grounds. Sex education also helps young people protect themselves from abuse, from disease, and from unwanted pregnancy. But modern censorship has been reducing the amount of sex education available to young people.

But what about 'hate speech'?

Who decides what qualifies as 'hate speech'? In Britain, it is illegal to incite people to any kind of violence, for racial or other reasons. But speech that actually encourages people to mistrust or hate their neighbours comes in many forms. We all notice it when crude words of racial hatred come from people in neo-Nazi garb, but the more refined speech of gentlemen in suits is both more insidious and more effective. And, once we have declared one word or phrase to be 'racist' or 'sexist', aren't we tacitly suggesting that everything else is fine?

If we try to ban certain kinds of ideas, we can never really challenge them in public debate. The real answer to bad speech is more speech.

- Feminists Against Censorship is a resource for educators, media, students, and others. We provide speakers, hold meetings, and offer guidance to those doing research or considering policies related to censorship, sexuality, feminism, and other civil liberties issues. We welcome supporters of all sexes. For more details about FAC contact: Feminists Against Censorship, BM FAC, London WC1N 3XX. Phone: (020) 8552-4405. Web site: www.fiawol.demon.co.uk/FAC/

© *Feminists Against Censorship*

R18 videos

The executive summary of a Consultation paper on the regulation of R18 videos

The Government maintains a firm commitment to the protection of children from unsuitable sexually explicit material. It takes the commonsense view that exposure to pornography of this type is potentially harmful to children generally. There is little conclusive evidence of harmful effects but formal research in this area – as in many others involving an assessment of the possible linkage between certain material and psychological damage or behavioural problems – is inherently difficult to carry out, particularly if it involves children. There is, however, evidence that sometimes this type of material is used by paedophiles to 'groom' children for sexual abuse. This paper explores a number of options to improve the protection of children from exposure to this type of material in the form of videos classified in the R (restricted) 18 category by the British Board of Film Classification (BBFC).

2. There are already a number of controls on the sale of this material through the Video Recordings Act 1984 which makes it an offence to supply R18 videos in premises other than a licensed sex shop and to those under the age of 18. However, although the legislative controls relating to the classification and sale of the videos remain the same as when the Act came into effect in 1984, the actual content of these videos has become more explicit. The BBFC have twice been successfully challenged by distributors on their decisions to refuse to classify a number of videos containing explicit scenes of intercourse and oral sex. The Video Appeals Committee (VAC) have found in favour of the appellants on both occasions. In May, the High Court dismissed the Board's application for judicial review of the VAC's judgement in the second appeal, finding that the VAC had acted reasonably in reaching their decision on the basis of the arguments put before them.

R18 videos

An introduction

1.1 The R (restricted) 18 classification certificate was introduced by the British Board of Film Censors (now Classification) (BBFC) following the introduction of the 1982 Local Government (Miscellaneous Provisions) Act which required the licensing of all cinema exhibitions operated for private gain, including those clubs which showed films containing more explicit sexual depictions than would be acceptable in the public adult – 18 – category. The classification has been used in the context of classifying sexually explicit videoworks for viewing in the home since the implementation of the Video Recordings Act 1984.

1.2 Although these videoworks contain material of a sexually explicit nature, they tend to be less explicit than those available in much of Europe. Under the most recent BBFC classification guidelines the composition of the videoworks is strictly controlled and all the explicit sexual acts shown (including sexual intercourse and oral sex) must be legal and consensual. In addition, the following content is not permitted under the BBFC guidelines:

- Any material which is in breach of the criminal law;
- Material likely to encourage an interest in abusive sexual activity (e.g. paedophilia, incest) which may include depictions involving adults role-playing as non-adults;
- The portrayal of any sexual activity, whether real or simulated, which involves lack of consent;
- The use of any form of physical restraint which prevents participants from withdrawing consent;
- The infliction of pain or physical harm, real or (in a sexual context) simulated; some allowance may be made for mild consensual activity;
- Any sexual threats or humiliations which do not form part of a clearly consenting role-playing game;
- Penetration by any object likely to cause actual harm or associated with violence;
- Activity which is degrading or dehumanising (e.g. bestiality, necrophilia)

3. Central to the Board's argument was their interpretation of the statutory responsibility placed

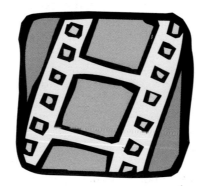

upon them – in terms of the protection of children – by Section 4 of the 1984 Video Recordings Act which requires them, among other things, to have regard to the harm to potential viewers which may be caused by the manner in which the video deals with criminal behaviour, drugs, violence, sexual activity or horrific behaviour. In view of the outcome of the judicial review and its implications for the Board's classification policy, the Home Secretary undertook to consider whether any additional steps could be taken to protect children from possible exposure to the sexually explicit material contained in R18 videos and to consult on the outcome.

4. This paper therefore explores a number of options to improve the protection of children in this area and also looks at proposals to bring the Video Appeals Committee into line with other, similar appeals bodies fulfilling an important public function, in terms of their recruitment and appointments system. This is a narrow subject focusing on the particular and immediate difficulties around R18 videos. It is not intended to cover the broader issue of controls on sexually explicit material in general in the United Kingdom, which is strictly regulated in comparison with many other countries. Nor does it explore the wider implications of the Internet or of

media convergence generally, which will be addressed in a Communications White Paper later this year.

5. The following options are examined in the paper:
- amendment to section 4A of the Video Recordings Act 1984 to reinforce the consideration the British Board of Film Classification must give to classifying material if there is a likelihood that children may be exposed to it (paragraphs 3.1 to 3.4);

- creation of new offences under the Video Recordings Act 1984, of showing a video classified as R18 to a child (under 16), allowing a child to watch an R18 video, and failing to take reasonable care to prevent a child from watching an R18 video (paragraphs 3.5 to 3.12);
- sentencing options including increasing the level of the fine for illegal supply of R18 videos, for example by mail order, to £20,000 as an exceptional statutory maximum (paragraphs 3.13 to 3.15); and
- modernisation of the existing procedures of the Video Appeals Committee or its re-establishment as a statutory body (paragraphs 3.16 to 3.21).

Film censor orders cuts under animal cruelty law

Film censors have taken the rare step of demanding cuts to an Oscar-nominated movie because of fears that birds were harmed during filming.

The British Board of Film Classification (BBFC) ordered the removal of a scene from *Before Night Falls*, a drama about the life of the Cuban poet Reinaldo Arenas, before awarding it a 15-certificate.

The ruling makes it the first new film in six years to be penalised under the Cinematograph Films (Animals) Act of 1937.

The offending scene shows a prison inmate capturing a bird. It seems to have been lassoed round the neck with a rope tied to the end of a stick.

As it flaps, fighting frantically to escape, it is pulled through a hole in the roof of the cell block. The BBFC says it is evidently distressed.

The American Humane Association (AHA), the US equivalent of the RSPCA, expressed concern. A BBFC

By Louise Jury, Media Correspondent

spokeswoman said: 'The assurances from the trainer/handler of the bird about the way the scene had been filmed were not consistent with what appears on screen. The BBFC, therefore, concluded that the scene should be cut.'

The film simulates a fight to the death between a rottweiler and a pit bull terrier in a Mexico City gambling den

Before Night Falls was made by the painter and film maker Julian Schnabel and won a best actor nomination in the Oscars for Javier Bardem, who plays Arenas.

However, the decision comes only weeks after another Oscar-nominated movie, *Amores Perros*, escaped cuts despite strong protests by the RSPCA.

The film simulates a fight to the death between a rottweiler and a pit bull terrier in a Mexico City gambling den and it had been thought it would fall foul of the law under a section outlawing the goading of animals for the camera.

Yet in that case the board was satisfied no animals were hurt or abused. The RSPCA criticised the ruling, saying it 'could contribute to the glamorisation of a horrifically cruel underground activity'.

The last new English language film to be cut under this legislation was *Run of the Country*, starring Albert Finney, in 1995, which contained scenes of cock fighting.

The board more frequently asks for scenes of animal cruelty to be removed from Asian films and videos.

Television and violence

Information from mediawatch-uk

Even if you watch just a few hours of TV a day, you can't miss the fact that violence is everywhere: terrestrial broadcast TV, cable or satellite. From Hollywood movies through soaps like *EastEnders* and *Brookside*, adult dramas like *Cracker* and even children's programmes like *Power Rangers*, realistic violence is the stuff of our leisure viewing.

Contrary to expectations of an improvement, the latest research report from National VALA, *More Cruelty and Violence 3* published in March 1997, shows TV violence worsening. Despite the horrific real life mowing down of most of a class of primary school children at Dunblane and the growing demands for stricter gun control that followed, shooting remains the commonest form of violence on screen.

Our analysis of a total of 246 films on the four terrestrial channels – BBC1, BBC2, ITV and Channel 4 – in 1996 detailed a massive 1,076 incidents involving firearms, 706 violent assaults and 376 incidents involving knives or other offensive weapons. 108 films were repeat screenings – already shown at least once on terrestrial TV and now allowed to be seen once again.

These findings are a shocking disgrace. The Broadcasting Authorities have done little to reduce screen violence despite mounting public and Parliamentary concern. Showing such films at later times seems to be the only action taken. The great – and the good – certainly know the power of television.

Our politicians use the TV to influence us to vote for them and to explain and to justify their policies. Our leading charities use it to persuade us to part with our money. They recognise that TV has a huge influence.

But the most committed believers in TV are the advertisers and their agencies. None of them would spend the millions and millions of pounds they invest in TV every year if it did not raise awareness of the message they are selling.

One alarming message that TV – not the advertisers! – increasingly sells us is that violence is acceptable. TV says violence is trivial, commonplace, everyday, mundane. It's part of life, normal. Part of our modern culture. And it can even be funny, in a sickly ironic way.

> *From Hollywood movies through soaps like EastEnders realistic violence is the stuff of our leisure viewing*

TV violence also teaches something even more corrupting – that intelligence is out, brute force is in. Morality is out. The cops are stupid, the criminals are the clever ones. It's a jungle out there, it's every man, woman and child for themselves, and it's 'cool'.

The Broadcasting Act 1990 stipulates, in Section 6(1)(a), that 'broadcasters should do all that they can to secure . . . that nothing is included in . . . programmes which offends against good taste or decency, or is likely to encourage or incite to crime or lead to disorder or be offensive to public feeling'.

This requirement also applies to the BBC through Clause 5(1)(d) of the 1996 Royal Charter. This is the letter of the law. It sounds good on paper. But can it be enforced?

Well-meaning senior broadcasters wishing to buck the trend and bring a climate of self-restraint and responsibility into their organisation must find the reality frustrating: neither the BBC nor the Independent Television Commission has the power to preview programmes or feature films, and stop them being shown if they fall short of requirements.

This is the case even when the provocative nature of the programme is widely publicised in advance so more people watch!

We live in an era of increased crimes of violence against the person or property, from child abuse to wife (or husband) battering, violence at football games, 'road rage', 'joy riding', vandalism and the mugging of the elderly or otherwise defenceless for a meagre handful of cash.

TV is our single biggest influence. Many young people have seen many thousands of crimes depicted on TV by the time they reach 18. It is not unreasonable to assume, on the balance of probability, that this

preoccupation with violence is bound to have harmful effects.

Violence on TV is glamorous and memorable. A scene lasting a few seconds – during a tiny part of the programme – may be remembered long after everything else in the story. Violence has a very contagious message and often produces an immediate effect.

Children imitate what they see. They turn it into games where others get hurt. Violence brutalises, it coarsens and depresses others. Its impact is overwhelming and corrupting.

Many scientifically conducted research studies have concluded that watching TV violence can have an effect on the behaviour and attitudes of everyone from Polynesian islanders to urban school children in Western countries.

In the UK the conclusions of these studies are often dismissed. Thankfully in the USA people across the political spectrum are beginning to accept their vitally important message. When will we wake up to it here?

Some TV producers, film directors and broadcasters laugh at our concerns about violence. They call any such outcry a 'kneejerk response'. But their entrenched view is similarly automatic. They say: 'It's realistic. It reflects reality. It's what the punters want. You don't have to watch it, do you? You can always turn off.'

But we don't have much choice, especially when these scenes are unexpected. We don't buy or rent our TVs to keep switching them off! You can't turn off your mind or fast forward something unpleasant that's being broadcast that very moment. Parents can't be there all the time to watch with their children during the hours devoted to children's programmes – nor should they have to.

TV, of course, is not the only problem. The UK's free market economy allows increasingly violent video games, computer games and videos to be sold or rented to impressionable young people. And there is the worrying development of the growing number of youth magazines pushing the idea that violence is actually trendy.

But staying with TV, the imminent explosion of new digital television channels presents a very serious threat to the regulation of programme content as required by the Broadcasting Act and the BBC's Royal Charter. Without Parliamentary intervention, the inescapable result of this expansion will be that responsibility for maintaining proper standards of good taste and decency will pass irretrievably out of the hands of the regulatory authorities and into those of the programme makers and service providers. And in National VALA's past experience, safeguarding good taste and decency – not to mention reducing violence – are not the programme makers' top priority!

The powers that be in this country have yet to actually do very much about it but at least broadcast violence, and its influence on children, in particular, is increasingly the subject of research and declarations of serious concern among our decision makers.

We hope their words lead to meaningful actions soon. In the meantime we cannot turn our backs on those affected, the vulnerable.

• The above information is an excerpt from *Television and Violence*, a booklet produced by mediawatch-uk. See page 41 for their address details.

© mediawatch-uk

Programme regulation

Information from the Independent Television Commission (ITC)

The ITC makes no programmes itself, nor does it broadcast or transmit programmes. But as the programme regulator, it sets the standards for programme content and ensures that the television companies licensed by the ITC comply with them. These standards are described in the ITC Programme Code and those sections of individual licences applying to programme provision. The Code includes guidelines covering:

• taste and decency, including strong language and sexual portrayal
• violence
• privacy
• impartiality
• charitable appeals
• religious programmes
• undue prominence for commercial products

The ITC also regulates to ensure quality and diversity are maintained on Channels 3, 4 and 5 and the Public Teletext Service and that, taken as a whole, television services appeal to a range of tastes and interests. (Regulation for services provided by satellite and cable is different from that for terrestrial services.)

In addition, each year, the ITC reviews the performance of Channels 3, 4, and 5 in relation to the terms of their licences and the licencees' own statements of programme quality and diversity.

The ITC has a wide range of powers at its disposal to enforce licence and Code requirements. Where a genuine mistake has been made in interpreting the Programme Code, or where the Code breach is not of a very serious nature, we will contact the television company concerned, offering guidance and making it clear that the offence should not be repeated.

In a more serious matter, we may issue a formal warning, require on-screen corrections or apologies, disallow a repeat or impose a fine. In the most extreme cases we can shorten the term of a licence or even withdraw it altogether.

Regulatory action and decisions are published, usually monthly, in our Programme Complaints and Interventions Report.

© Independent Television Commission (ITC)

Private lives, cutting edges

In this day and age, do we really need to have a censor?

By Nigella Lawson

Is there anyone who truly believes that seeing a violent film is going to make them violent? No – but we all fear the effect it has on others. Of course, our fears are – as they should be – concerned mostly with the vulnerable young, and that certainly seems to be the drive behind the latest rethink of film-categorisation and censorship policy.

Yet however well intentioned any discussion of censorship rules or guidance, there is an inherent problem. Our society is violent. Not as violent as it has been (though there wasn't the mass entertainment business around to exploit it in such glorious Technicolor), but we do seem to enjoy violence and no amount of censorship can have any impact on that.

While I can understand the primitive bloodlust that lies behind the desire to see as much detailed, hideously realistic violence in the name of entertainment as possible, I am more disturbed by the impulse itself than its screen manifestation. And this is not because I feel there is a danger of our being actively corrupted: it's that our appetite for it is a sign of our prior corruption. Perhaps our untroubled engagement with the violent and the horrific is the natural reaction of a coddled generation: we haven't witnessed war or had to go off to fight. Our lives are protected and sanitised, and the result is that while we insist on trying to make the world less randomly dangerous than it ever can be, we are intent on immersing ourselves in lurid acts of violence that the age we live in has otherwise spared us.

The drug issue is rather different. There are few parents of teenage or less-than-teenage children who aren't terrified at the availability and ubiquity of drugs but we seem to think the way to protect our children from them is to prevent them from seeing the harm they can do. *Trainspotting* was condemned as a glamorisation of drug-taking; but if anything, it showed how seedy, how painful, how destructive a heroin habit could be. Of course, it also showed why people would want to be lost in a drug-fuelled landscape. What is wrong with that? How does it help to pretend life is other than it is? More salient, how does it offer protection?

> *Our society is violent. Not as violent as it has been, but we do seem to enjoy violence and no amount of censorship can have any impact on that*

In truth, I don't understand how the president of the British Board of Film Censors, Andreas Whittam Smith, could say, and believe it to be responsible: 'I think if *Pulp Fiction* were to come to us for the first time now, we would look at that scene where we see John Travolta in a car, high on heroin with a little more concern than we expressed two or three years ago.' Does he really think excising that scene would have any impact on heroin use among cinema-goers?

If this seems inconsistent – in that I have declared my distaste for screen violence to have no basis in the belief that it might incite further public violence – it is because the two areas of concern are disparate. But the sort of violence people pay to go and see is cartoon-violence. It's for amusement. It's not really that much different from the enjoyment taken in a television series such as *Casualty*, which is not shocking or repellent, but does in the same way make one wonder about what kind of people we are that we take so much pleasure in viewing people even play-acting distress, pain, suffering, the rest. In part, I envy those whose lives are so untouched by personal catastrophe that they feel impelled to make up the shortfall cinematically or on television. But the fact that people take drugs, and

ACKNOWLEDGEMENTS

While every care has been taken to trace and acknowledge copyright, the publisher tenders its apology for any accidental infringement or where copyright has proved untraceable. The publisher would be pleased to come to a suitable arrangement in any such case with the rightful owner.

Chapter One: The Debate

Making sense of censorship, © Family and Youth Concern, *Film censor to stop playing nanny*, © Guardian Newspapers Limited 2001, *Classification guidelines*, © British Board of Film Classification (BBFC), *What should 12-year-olds be trusted to see?*, © 2001 Independent Newspaper (UK) Ltd, *Campaign against censorship*, © Campaign Against Censorship, *The scary truth about horror movies*, © Guardian Newspapers Limited 2001, *Can the net stay free?*, © Guardian Newspapers Limited 2000, *Patrolling the internet*, © Guardian Newspapers Limited 2000, *Access denied*, © Index on Censorship, *Web inventor denounces net censorship*, © Guardian Newspapers Limited 2000, *New age rating symbols for computer games*, © The European Leisure Software Publishers' Association (ELSPA), *Game classifications*, © Video Standards Council (VSC), *School massacre families to sue creators of violent games*, © 2001 Independent Newspaper (UK) Ltd, *Reflecting community values*, © The Broadcasting Standards Commission, *The Broadcasting Standards Commission*, © The Broadcasting Standards Commission.

Chapter Two: Sex and Violence

The main concerns, © British Board of Film Classification (BBFC), *Film sex rules to be eased*, © Telegraph Group Limited, London 2000, *Sense and sensibilities*, © British Board of Film Classification (BBFC), *The classifications*, © British Board of Film Classification (BBFC), *Child guinea pigs to view 'adult' film scenes*, © 2001 Independent Newspaper (UK) Ltd, *'We need to know about these things', they are part of life'*, © 2001 Independent Newspaper (UK) Ltd, *Television and sex*, © mediawatch-uk, *TV film viewers want information not censorship*, © Guardian Newspapers Limited 2000, *More sex please, we're British filmgoers*, © Guardian Newspapers Limited 2000, *Do you really want more censorship?*, © Feminists Against Censorship, *R18 videos*, © Crown copyright is reproduced with the permission of the Controller of Her Majesty's Stationery Office (HMSO), *Film censor orders cuts under animal cruelty law*, © 2001 Independent Newspaper (UK) Ltd, *Television and violence*, © mediawatch-uk, *Programme regulation*, © Independent Television Commission (ITC), *Private lives, cutting edges*, © Guardian Newspapers Limited 2000, *Delete expletives?*, © Broadcasting Standards Commission (BSC), *'Super watchdog' for TV, radio and the web*, © Telegraph Group Limited, London 2001.

Photographs and illustrations:

Pages 1, 4, 24: Pumpkin House, pages 2, 6, 14, 17, 19, 22, 25, 30, 35, 37: Simon Kneebone.

Craig Donnellan
Cambridge
September, 2001